▶ Forensic Authorship Analysis and the World Wide Web

DOI: 10.1057/9781137413758.0001

Other Palgrave Pivot titles

Karen Rich: Interviewing Rape Victims: Practice and Policy Issues in an International Context

Vieten M. Ulrike (editor): Revisiting Iris Marionyoung on Normalisation, Inclusion and Democracy

Fuchaka Waswa, Christine Ruth Saru Kilalo, and Dominic Mwambi Mwasaru: Sustainable Community Development: Dilemma of Options in Kenya

Giovanni Barone Adesi: Simulating Security Returns: A Filtered Historical Simulation Approach

Daniel Briggs and Dorina Dobre: Culture and Immigration in Context: An Ethnography of Romanian Migrant Workers in London

Toswell, M.J.: Borges the Unacknowledged Medievalist

Lack, Anthony: Martin Heidegger on Technology, Ecology, and the Arts

Carlos A. Scolari, Paolo Bertetti and Matthew Freeman: Transmedia Archaeology: Storytelling in the Borderlines of Science Fiction, Comics and Pulp Magazines

Judy Rohrer: Queering the Biopolitics of Citizenship in the Age of Obama

Paul Jackson and Anton Shekhovtsov: The Post-War Anglo-American Far Right: A Special Relationship of Hate

Elliot D. Cohen: Technology of Oppression: Preserving Freedom and Dignity in an Age of Mass, Warrantless Surveillance

Ilan Alon (editor): Social Franchising

Richard Michael O'Meara: Governing Military Technologies in the 21st Century: Ethics and Operations

Thomas Birtchnell and William Hoyle: 3D Printing for Development in the Global South: The 3D4D Challenge

David Fitzgerald and David Ryan: Obama, US Foreign Policy and the Dilemmas of Intervention

Lars Elleström: Media Transformation: The Transfer of Media Characteristics Among Media

Claudio Povolo: The Novelist and the Archivist: Fiction and History in Alessandro Manzoni's The Betrothed

Gerbrand Tholen: The Changing Nature of the Graduate Labour Market: Media, Policy and Political Discourses in the UK

Aaron Stoller: Knowing and Learning as Creative Action: A Reexamination of the Epistemological Foundations of Education

Carl Packman: Payday Lending: Global Growth of the High-Cost Credit Market

Lisa Lau and Om Prakash Dwivedi: Re-Orientalism and Indian Writing in English

Chapman Rackaway: Communicating Politics Online

G. Douglas Atkins: T.S. Eliot's Christmas Poems: An Essay in Writing-as-Reading and Other "Impossible Unions"

Marsha Berry and Mark Schleser: Mobile Media Making in an Age of Smartphones

DOI: 10.1057/9781137413758.0001

palgrave▸pivot

Forensic Authorship Analysis and the World Wide Web

Samuel Larner
University of Central Lancashire, UK

DOI: 10.1057/9781137413758.0001

First published 2014 by
PALGRAVE MACMILLAN

Palgrave Macmillan in the UK is an imprint of Macmillan Publishers Limited,
registered in England, company number 785998, of Houndmills, Basingstoke,
Hampshire RG21 6XS.

Palgrave Macmillan in the US is a division of St Martin's Press LLC,
175 Fifth Avenue, New York, NY 10010.

Palgrave Macmillan is the global academic imprint of the above companies
and has companies and representatives throughout the world.

Palgrave® and Macmillan® are registered trademarks in the United States,
the United Kingdom, Europe and other countries.

ISBN: 978-1-137-41376-5   EPUB
ISBN: 978-1-137-41375-8   PDF
ISBN: 978-1-137-41374-1   Hardback

A catalogue record for this book is available from the British Library.

A catalog record for this book is available from the Library of Congress.

www.palgrave.com/pivot

DOI: 10.1057/9781137413758

For Simon and Penny

DOI: 10.1057/9781137413758.0001

Contents

DOI: 10.1057/9781137413758.0001

DOI: 10.1057/9781137413758.0001

Acknowledgements

This research has been conducted over a ten-year period, starting in 2004 and concluding in 2014. Over this period, I have talked about my research with several people who offered useful advice. In particular I would like to thank Janet Cotterill for her insightful comments on the first stages of this research, which were carried out in 2004 at Cardiff University, and Mandip Bains for being a superb friend and sounding board for my ideas.

▶ I would also like to thank my colleagues and friends at the University of Central Lancashire for their support and encouragement. I am particularly grateful to my Dean, Isabel Donnelly, for supporting my sabbatical application so that I could complete this work, and my colleagues in the Linguistics team who covered my absence. I am especially grateful to Dawn Archer for her enthusiasm and guidance, and Paul Seager for his advice and for keeping me on track with my writing. I owe my thanks to Beth Richardson who kindly covered some of my teaching which allowed me to push ahead with my writing. Thanks also to Libby Forrest and Rebecca Brennan at Palgrave Macmillan for expertly guiding me through the publication process.

In addition, there are some very important people to thank who kept things ticking over at home whilst I was locked away in my study. Terry and Lynne Larner have always been wonderful parents, but over the past 12

DOI: 10.1057/9781137413758.0002

months in particular have offered a great deal of support and kindness. Thank you very much for helping me and Simon when we needed it the most.

And finally, my biggest thanks goes to Simon Larner for his constant support and reassurance, and Penny for sensing when I needed cuddles.

DOI: 10.1057/9781137413758.0002

palgrave▶**pivot**

www.palgrave.com/pivot

1
Introduction: The UNABOM Investigation

Abstract: *Increasingly, forensic linguists are using the web to generate evidence in cases of forensic authorship analysis. A striking example of this occurred during the trial of the Unabomber – a prolific serial bomber – when the web was searched to determine the distinctiveness of a set of idiolectal co-selections. However, to date, questions have not been asked about whether the web can be used reliably in forensic contexts. Therefore, using the Unabomber trial evidence as a case study, this chapter discusses the notion of idiolect and introduces research which explores two issues: (1) whether idiolectal co-selections can be used as a marker of authorship, and (2) whether the web is reliable enough to be used to produce forensic evidence.*

Keywords: authorship attribution; idiolect; idiolectal co-selections; Unabomber; web corpus

Larner, Samuel. *Forensic Authorship Analysis and the World Wide Web.* Basingstoke: Palgrave Macmillan, 2014. DOI: 10.1057/9781137413758.0003.

Linguists are increasingly utilising the world wide web (henceforth "web"[1]) as a corpus for research purposes (Volk, 2002) and, given that many linguists acknowledge corpus linguistics as a mainstream methodology (Lindquist & Levin, 2000), coupled with the importance of corpus linguistics methods in the field of forensic linguistics (Coulthard, 1994; Hänlein, 1999; Solan & Tiersma, 2004; Woolls & Coulthard, 1998), it stands to reason that forensic linguists increasingly turn to the web for investigative and evidential purposes. This is particularly the case for forensic authorship analysis – determining the author of a document whose authorship is contested, such as in detecting plagiarism and collusion, attributing a criminal text to an author from a list of potential authors, or profiling an unknown author based on linguistic characteristics. In such cases, the linguist may use the web to show the distinctiveness or rarity of particular words and phrases (Coulthard, 2004).

A striking example of this occurred during the trial of Theodore Kaczynski, a prolific American serial bomber. During the period of May 1978 to April 1995, a total of 16 bombing incidents occurred, initially targeted at individuals connected to universities and the airline industry. These specific targets led the FBI to codename the investigation UNABOM. As a result of the bombing campaign, three people were killed and many more were injured. In June 1995, *The New York Times*, *The Washington Post*, *Penthouse*, and *Scientific American* (as well as a Professor of Sociology at the University of California at Berkeley) received a manuscript – a terrorist's manifesto purportedly written by the Unabomber – entitled *An industrial society and its future*. Along with the manuscript was a deal: if the manuscript was published in full, the bombing would stop. *The Washington Post* eventually published the manuscript in September 1995 (Fitzgerald, 2004).

Upon reading an internet version of the published manifesto, Linda Patrik became unnerved. Although she had never met her brother-in-law, there was something about the text that seemed familiar. She asked her husband, David Kaczynski, to read the publication and urged him to compare it with her brother-in-law's writings. David sceptically complied, but started to suspect that his older brother, Theodore, may indeed be the Unabomber. The occurrence of one phrase in particular convinced him: *cool-headed logicians*. David recalled his brother "using that distinctive term on numerous occasions" (Fitzgerald, 2004: 208) and as a result, he contacted the FBI. To assist with the investigation, the Kaczynski family made available many documents known to have been written by Theodore for comparative analysis with the manifesto (p. 208).

James Fitzgerald of the FBI Behavioral Analysis Unit led a team of FBI agents and analysts in the comparative analysis of writings known to have been authored by the Unabomber (including so-called ruse letters which incited recipients to open accompanying bombing devices sent through the mail, ideological letters which outlined the Unabomber's rationale for the bombing campaign, brokering letters in which the Unabomber tried to get the manifesto published, and of course the manifesto itself) with writings known to have been authored by Kaczynski (which included, amongst others, Kaczynski's doctoral thesis, personal letters, and short stories) (Fitzgerald, 2004). In April 1996, after reviewing all of the evidence, including the report produced by the comparative analysis team, a federal judge signed a warrant to search Kaczynski's cabin in Montana. The FBI arrested Kaczynski at his home, whereupon they found "a virtual treasure trove of evidentiary materials" (p. 215) including a fully assembled bomb and numerous bomb parts.

In preparation for the trial, Kaczynski's defence team attempted to undermine the basis on which the search warrant had been obtained: "If they could get a ruling from the judge during the pre-trial stage that the search warrant was obtained by the FBI improperly, and that there was not enough probable cause to support the search, the entire case against Kaczynski could conceivably be dismissed" (Fitzgerald, 2004: 216). The comparative analysis team's report came under scrutiny by the defence's expert witness, Robin Lakoff, who outlined seven areas of error, and opined that the claims of common authorship between the known writings of the Unabomber and the known writings of Theodore Kackzynski were "untenable and unreliable at best" (Fitzgerald, 2004: 217). On the other hand, the prosecution's expert witness, Donald Foster, concluded that "Fitzgerald had cautiously understated the case for common authorship" (Foster, 2001: 107). According to Coulthard (2000), Lakoff argued that many of the lexical items which were shared across both groups of texts could "quite easily occur in any argumentative text" (p. 281) and were therefore not indicative of common authorship between the Unabomber's terrorist manifesto and Kaczynski's known writings. In particular, 12 words and phrases were selected for exemplification: *at any rate, clearly, in practice, gotten, more or less, moreover, on the other hand, presumably, propaganda, thereabouts,* and lexemes derived from the lemmas *argu* and *propos* (p. 281).

DOI: 10.1057/9781137413758.0003

To counter the proposal that such words and phrases could occur in any similar text, Coulthard (2000) reports that the web was searched and approximately three million documents were found which included at least one or more of the 12 lexical items. However, when the search was limited to finding only documents which contained all 12 lexical items, only 69 documents were identified and each of these documents was an online copy of the terrorist manifesto (p. 282). Coulthard concludes of this evidence that "a writer's combinations of lexical choices are more unique, diagnostic or idiolectal than people have so far been willing to believe" (p. 282). Furthermore, Coulthard (2004) argues that this evidence is "a powerful example of the idiolectal habit of co-selection and an illustration of the consequent forensic possibilities that idiolectal co-selection affords for authorship attribution" (p. 433).[2]

In order to judge this evidence as "powerful", two assertions must firstly be accepted: (1) that idiolectal co-selection – that is, words which taken in combination appear to characterise an individual author's linguistic style – is a useful marker of authorship; and (2) that the web is a valid and reliable corpus for producing forensic evidence. As will become clear in Section 1.3, the aim of this research is to test empirically both of these assertions, and since testing both assertions rests on the notion of idiolect and the use of lexis as a marker of authorship, it is firstly necessary to discuss both before setting out the scope of this research.

1.1   Idiolect

Although the term *idiolect* was first coined by Bloch (1948), Sapir (1927) laid the groundwork in his discussion of the relationship between speech and personality. Sapir outlined five levels of speech that were indexical of individual personality including voice, dynamics, pronunciation, vocabulary, and style. Of these, *vocabulary* and *style* are the most relevant precursors to the concept of idiolect. Sapir argued of vocabulary that:

> We do not all speak alike. There are certain words which some of us never use. There are other, favorite, words which we are always using... Individual variation exists, but it can properly be appraised only with reference to the social norm. Sometimes we choose words because we like them; sometimes we slight words because they bore or annoy or terrify us. We are not going to be caught by them. All in all, there is room for much subtle analysis in the determination of the social and individual significance of words. (p. 903)

DOI: 10.1057/9781137413758.0003

Here, Sapir clearly draws out the potential for individual variation at the lexical level (further considered in Section 1.2) and the complex relationship between the individual and society, which is further exemplified through his consideration of individual style:

> We all have our individual styles in both conversation and considered address, and they are never the arbitrary and casual things we think them to be. There is always an individual method, however poorly developed, of arranging words into groups and of working these up into larger units. It would be a very complicated problem to disentangle the social and individual determinants of style, but it is a theoretically possible one. (pp. 903–4)

Some linguists have given a more prominent place to writing alongside speech than Sapir (e.g. Coulthard, 2004) whilst for others, the term "style" is instead a recognised term for "idiolect in writing" (e.g. Kredens, 2002). In the context of this research, idiolect should be understood to include written language.

A good early definition for the discussion of idiolect is Hockett's (1958): "the totality of speech habits of a single person at a given time constitutes an idiolect" (p. 321). Hockett's definition raises two issues: potentially, one might need to observe and catalogue every single speech habit before one could fully characterise an individual's idiolect, and secondly that idiolect will change over time. In so far as *totality* means *complete* and *entire*, Hockett appears to suggest that idiolect is the entire repertoire of speech habits available to a single person. However, it is impossible to collect a totality, although for Hockett's purposes this would not have been an issue. In fact, in a later paragraph, Hockett notes that the entire idiolect cannot be observed, only examples of the linguistic output that it generates (1958: 322). In other words, rather than being able to observe the totality of habits, all that the linguist can observe is what a speaker or writer actually does at the particular point of observation.

The second implication of Hockett's definition, that idiolectal features can only be described *at a given time*, implies that idiolect is organic and evolutionary in nature and will differ when observed at different times. This raises the question of by how much and whether the difference is significant. Related to this is the issue of the rate at which such change occurs, a question which so far has received no definitive answer with the exception of Bel et al. (2012) who show that the use of bigrams and trigrams do not vary substantially across a span of between six and ten years for individual authors (ages unknown), indicating that this

DOI: 10.1057/9781137413758.0003

feature remains sufficiently stable for this limited period of time at least. Corroborative evidence is provided by Barlow (2010) who found that bigrams were used consistently over the shorter period of one year in the spoken language of White House Press Secretaries. The problem with such a definition for forensic purposes is that not only would the idiolect of one individual differ from that of another (as assumed in authorship attribution, although cf. Grant (2010) for an alternative view on the importance of idiolect for forensic purposes), but would also be subject to variation between the same individual when observed at different points. This would make the comparison of documents in the forensic context very difficult because Known Documents (those documents whose authorship is attested, henceforth KD) are rarely authored at the same time as each other or as the Questioned Documents (those documents whose authorship is unknown and under suspicion, henceforth QD).

Sixty years later, Louwerse (2004) claimed that writers "implicitly leave their signature in the document they write" and that idiolects "are person-dependent similarities in language use" (p. 207). He explains that if idiolect exists, texts composed by one author will show more similarities in language than texts composed by different authors (p. 207). However, a potential problem arises in relation to Hockett's definition. Louwerse states that similarities between texts produced by one author will be greater than texts produced by different authors. Hockett proposes that idiolect will change over time. Unless the individual signatures upon which Louwerse's definition relies remain static, the similarities between two pieces of writing by the same individual at different times could be no greater than the similarities between two individuals with similar linguistic backgrounds (a common assumption, e.g. Loakes, 2006). It seems then that the temporal dimension could indeed be a confounding variable in forensic authorship attribution. Through examining a third definition of idiolect, a clearer picture may be gained.

Coulthard (2004) also says that "every native speaker has their own distinct and individual version of the language they speak and write, their own *idiolect*" and that "this *idiolect* will manifest itself through distinctive and idiosyncratic choices in texts" (pp. 431–2, original emphasis). The main difference here is between what Coulthard refers to as *choice* and what Hockett refers to as *habit*. Insofar as *choice* implies conscious decision, *habit* implies an involuntary behaviour pattern. If idiolect is based on habit, it is reasonable to argue that a person's linguistic patterns will remain constant, until such a time when that habit is changed. In this scenario, texts produced during a period when the habit remains the same should be comparable. Choice, however, is more volatile and dependent on many extra-linguistic factors (e.g. mood of the individual, genre of the text, audience of the text, time available to compose the text, and indeed recency) as well as conscious attempts to disguise identity. As such, any features of language that are subject to choice could result in differences between texts produced by the same author, regardless of when they were authored.

These three definitions, somewhat representative of the many that could have been reviewed (e.g. Labov, 1972; Trudgill, 1974, 2003; Wardhaugh, 2006) capture between them the key issue for authorship attribution, namely, the extent to which an individual's idiolect really is a reliable signature irrespective of stylistic choice and change over time. However, it is readily acknowledged that the theory of idiolect, to date, lacks empirical investigation (e.g. Kredens, 2001, 2002; Louwerse, 2004; Kniffka, 2007), and, as discussed above, the totality of linguistic habits for each person can never fully be observed. This point is echoed by Coulthard (2004) who says that "any linguistic sample, even a very large one, provides only very partial information about its creator's idiolect" (p. 432), so it remains a largely theoretical notion. In light of its theoretical basis, it is now necessary to be explicit about how idiolect will be understood and applied in this research. From reviewing the definitions of idiolect provided by Hockett (1958), Louwerse (2004), and Coulthard (2004), the consensus seems to be that either choice, habit, or both are intrinsically linked to idiolect. The definition to be used in this research is therefore as follows:

> Determined and conditioned by a wide and immeasurable range of biological, sociological, cognitive and environmental factors (including *inter alia* age, IQ, occupation, friendship networks, language contact), idiolect is the combination of language choices (planned features) and habits (subconscious features) made by an individual, the sum of which creates a distinctive, albeit oftentimes overlapping, range of choices and habits from another individual. (Tomblin, 2013: 35)

In this conceptualisation of idiolect, the goal of the forensic linguist is to identify those features of idiolect which overlap less with others in order to demonstrate the similarity or difference between a series of authors. It will not be possible to determine in this research what constitutes a choice and what constitutes a habit, but one might surmise that a feature such as using a specific lexical item to mark identity (such as youth vernacular words

DOI: 10.1057/9781137413758.0003

commonly found in the school playground) may be a choice whereas final /g/ clipping in the case of spoken language may be a habit. Furthermore, choices and habits should be viewed as being on the same cline. A feature may start out as being a conscious choice but over time moves into being a habit. An example may be when a person moves to a new geographical region and starts to use a dialectal term of endearment in order to fit in but over time more naturally and automatically uses that term. Any reference to idiolect in the remainder of this research should be understood against this definition. As mentioned at the start of this section with reference to Sapir (1927), words are assumed to be idiolectal and therefore can be used as a marker of authorship – that is, they have the ability to distinguish texts written by the same author or by different authors.

1.2   Lexis as a marker of authorship

Gibbons (2003) claims that particular words may contribute to identifying an author (p. 303), as does Winter (1996) who claims that vocabulary should not only be the starting point when differentiating authors, but "should be the standard approach to any linguistic analysis which compares texts" (p. 165). Coulthard (1994) also highlights the benefit of analysing documents for "unlikely vocabulary choices" (p. 38), particularly in contested police statements, and there is an established tradition of using lexis as a marker of authorship in terms of both the frequency of function words (e.g. Bagavandas & Manimannon, 2008) and vocabulary richness (e.g. Baker, 1988; Chaski, 2001; Grieve, 2007; Holmes & Forsyth, 1995; Mosteller & Wallace, 1963), although opinions vary over which aspects of lexis are the most fruitful to explore. For instance, Foster (2001) argues that an accepted measure of attributional evidence is the frequency of function words whereas Johnson (1997), in the area of plagiarism at least, suggests that as the binding links in a sentence that cannot easily be disposed with (perhaps with the exception of telegrams, cf. Stubbs, 2002), function words should potentially increase with length rather than idiolectal linguistic behaviour:

> Closed items, being from a small closed set of vocabulary, are relatively stable whoever the writer or whatever the text. It is in lexical choices that writers distinguish themselves as individuals. (pp. 220–1)

Moreover, Stubbs (2002) comments that there is a very high correlation between the top 100 most frequent words and the amount of those which are function words (p. 227). It therefore seems that focussing on content word types holds potential to mark out texts as written by the same author or between different authors. Hoover (2003) highlights a potential problem though, that "authors normally learn new words. Authors also forget words, or stop using them" (p. 157). In this case, lexis may not be a useful marker of authorship. However, given that lexis was used as a marker of authorship in the UNABOM investigation, and given that lexis is generally an accepted marker of authorship in the field of forensic linguistics, so too will it be used in the present research, whilst acknowledging that focussing on the open class set of lexical items is not necessarily the most effective marker of authorship, nor indeed the only marker of authorship.

1.3   Central research question and research aims

When Foster (2001) analysed the anonymously written novel *Primary Colours* for its likely author, he identified the 400 least common words in the book and searched a corpus of candidate authors' texts for close vocabulary matches (p. 59). Foster commented that a "computer-assisted search failed to deliver a single plausible suspect" (p. 60). This was until he was sent more examples of texts from suspect authors. This raises the question of whether a larger database in terms of comparison materials from candidate authors increases the likelihood of establishing common authorship between the QDs and KDs. If so, searching a large database like the web – possibly the largest potential database of authors – seems like a plausible place to search for evidence of authorship, as Coulthard (2000) reports it being used during the UNABOM trial. However, Hoover (2003) argues in contrast to Foster (2001) that as more texts are added into a corpus where vocabulary is being investigated, accuracy is actually reduced. Hoover claims that authorship determined in this way "is possible only with a small and extremely various group of texts" (p. 170), which if correct, would discount the web as a resource.

Using lexis as a marker of authorship and the UNABOM investigation as a case study, this research aims to evaluate the effectiveness of using the web to generate evidence of idiolectal co-selection in cases of forensic authorship analysis. Whilst the aim of this research is not to discredit any of the analysis carried out during the UNABOM trial, it does seek to evaluate the effectiveness and reliability of using the web in

DOI: 10.1057/9781137413758.0003

this way. The UNABOM analysis – searching the web for 12 words and phrases – was conducted in the late 1990s and, undoubtedly, the web has undergone massive growth since this initial analysis. This raises the question of whether the web is reliable as a tool, given that it is not static and is constantly evolving (Fielden & Kuntz, 2002) and whether the same results can be obtained if the analysis is repeated. Additionally, both Woolls and Coulthard (1998) and Johnson (1997) highlight that shared lexis between documents is generally indicative of plagiarism. Therefore, it is possible that by searching the web for lexis shared across documents and finding the same 12 lexical items in different versions of the Unabomber's terrorist manifesto may have been more akin to the methods used in plagiarism detection, rather than demonstrating the power of idiolectal co-selection. It is argued here that more persuasive evidence of idiolectal co-selection would have been provided if other documents written by Kaczynski, and Kaczynski alone, had been identified on the web alongside the terrorist manifesto, using the combination of 12 lexical items as a search query. This would have demonstrated consistent use of those 12 lexical items across a series of texts for one author.

In this research, two key questions are addressed: (1) Can idiolectal co-selections be used as a marker of authorship? and (2) Is the web reliable enough to be used as evidence of authorship in forensic contexts? The aims of the research are as follows:

1   To develop a method for isolating sets of idiolectal co-selections for authors;
2   To use the web to evaluate the distinctiveness of each set of idiolectal co-selections;
3   To attempt to attribute documents to their authors based on idiolectal co-selections using the web; and
4   To evaluate the web as a tool for the forensic linguist.

1.4   Overview of the research

This research is divided into five chapters and, following this introductory chapter, Chapter 2 sets out the issues relating to the use of the web as a corpus in forensic investigations. Included in Chapter 2 are sections which address the nature of the web and search engines since it is only through an understanding of how searches are carried out and what they

DOI: 10.1057/9781137413758.0003

actually search, that potential limitations can be identified. However, it should be noted that this research is aimed at those linguists who use the web as a corpus to investigate patterns of language use, particularly those who use such evidence in forensic contexts. As such, a basic understanding of forensic linguistics and especially authorship analysis, and corpus linguistics is presumed. Furthermore, an understanding of how web searches operate is provided in Chapter 2, but this description has been necessarily simplified and will not be sufficient for specialists in this area seeking technical detail. Chapters 3 and 4 describe empirical research. The empirical research in Chapter 3 explores whether idiolectal co-selections can firstly be identified in a text and in order to do this, a novel method for identifying idiolectal co-selections is described. The web is then used to assess the distinctiveness of idiolectal co-selections, and the research is repeated over a seven day and ten year period, using different search techniques and engines in order to assess the reliability of the results. In this chapter, two documents are used for the analysis in a scenario where there are no candidate authors – in other words, no comparison documents are available. In Chapter 4, the same methods are used to determine sets of idiolectal co-selections for authors. However, in this chapter only one QD is under investigation, which is compared against documents written by three authors in order to assess whether evidence of authorship is stronger when candidate authors are available, compared to Chapter 3. Chapter 5 concludes this research by discussing the findings from Chapters 3 and 4, particularly in light of the demands of forensic evidence.

Notes

1 Traditionally, treating *internet* and *web* as proper nouns emphasised their novelty, whereas the technology is now so embedded in our daily practices that such emphasis is outdated. Therefore, following the convention of Wired.com (2004, cited in Blum, 2012: 106), *internet* and *web* will not be capitalised in this work, with the exception of direct quotations where the original formatting will be preserved.

2 Fitzgerald did not use the web in this way during the UNABOM investigation (personal communication, 14 April 2005) and neither Fitzgerald (2004) nor Foster (2001) report on this aspect of the investigation.

DOI: 10.1057/9781137413758.0003

2

The Web as Corpus and Authorship Attribution

Abstract: *In order to understand the potential limitations and problems with using the web as a corpus during forensic investigations, key issues covered in this chapter include a description of the web and how it is searched using commercial search engines. The reliability of search engines is then discussed with evidence suggesting that whilst search engine results can be unstable, to some extent they appear to be reliable. Issues in using the web as a corpus, focussing particularly on size and representativeness are discussed, before characterising the web as a raw, general corpus. The chapter concludes by discussing the issues raised from the specific perspective of a forensic linguist.*

Keywords: authorship analysis; forensic linguistics; search engines; web corpus

Larner, Samuel. *Forensic Authorship Analysis and the World Wide Web*. Basingstoke: Palgrave Macmillan, 2014. DOI: 10.1057/9781137413758.0004.

DOI: 10.1057/9781137413758.0004

Čermák (2002) explains that when it comes to corpus linguistics, "[w]hat is really needed is a steady increase and perpetual growth of even, by present standards, very large corpora of billions of words, which should be as much representative as possible" (p. 267) and it is clear why linguists should turn to the web as a corpus, given its immense size. Likewise, writing in 1991, Leech argued that due to copyright and legal restrictions, "the concept of a corpus which is in the public domain – available unconditionally for all users – does not so far exist, except for texts too old to be in copyright" (p. 11). A similar point was made almost a decade later by Lindquist and Levin (2000) who suggested that scholars are limited in the corpora that they can use because of economic, financial and copyright restrictions, the result being that research is sometimes conducted with insufficient material which is not representative (p. 201). However, the web appears to have overcome these restrictions. Kilgarriff and Grefenstette (2003) explain that "[t]he Web is immense, free and available by mouse click. It contains hundreds of billions of words of text" (p. 333), a point which is also made by Blair, Urland and Ma (2002):

> The Internet is ubiquitous and search engines are generally free sites, making issues of availability and cost nearly irrelevant. Moreover, the Internet is relatively comprehensive, including academic texts, commercial and personal information, and records from newsgroup postings. (p. 287)

Furthermore, Kilgarriff and Grefenstette (2003) argue that because the web is so big, free and "instantly available" (p. 333) use of the web as a source of language data is becoming increasingly common for linguists, thereby implying that what was true for Leech (1991) is now perhaps more of a reality. Therefore, the web appears to have realised Leech's vision of third-generation corpora which he predicted would be measured in hundreds of millions of words and would exploit the technologies of computer text processing: "huge amounts of machine-readable text [will] become available as a by-product of modern electronic communication systems" (1991: 10).

Since the web is used – by many people – on a daily basis for a variety of reasons, the task of searching can be taken for granted; that is, questions are not always asked about what is actually being searched and how, because for most of us searching the web is second nature. It may be that having such easy access to a huge source of language data outweighs some of the potential limitations of searching the web. Therefore, in order to begin evaluating the reliability of the web in cases of authorship

DOI: 10.1057/9781137413758.0004

attribution, this chapter firstly describes what the web actually is, taking into account its size and composition. The nature of search engines is then explored by considering how they operate, what their priorities are, and crucially whether their priorities conflict with those of a linguist. A discussion regarding the reliability of searching the web using search engines will follow, at which point a consideration of the web as a corpus will be presented. This chapter will conclude by considering all of the issues raised from the specific perspective of a forensic linguist in order to identify the key potential problems with using evidence generated from the web in order to inform the empirical work described in Chapters 3 and 4.

2.1   The web

For many people, there is little distinction between the terms *web* and *internet*. However, such a distinction does exist. Broadly speaking, the *internet* refers to something tangible – a physical connection of wires which connects millions of computers throughout the world to one another (Levene, 2010: 1). The *web*, by contrast, is a "virtual global network" (p. 1) and comprises, in broad terms, anything that can be viewed using a standard web browser. Naughton (2012) defines the web as "a vast store of online information in the form of 'pages' of varying sizes which are connected to one another via clickable links" (p. 210). Therefore, the actual transmission of data, e-mails and uploading and downloading of files relies on an internet connection rather than using the web (although increasingly these parameters are becoming blurred through the use of, for instance, web-based e-mail services such as *Hotmail* and cloud-based file storage such as *Microsoft OneDrive*). In other words, to use the web, an internet connection is required, but having an internet connection does not necessarily mean surfing the web. Naughton (2012) explains that as it was originally created, the web consisted of fixed pages which facilitated the global sharing of information. In this way, the web was "a world-wide repository of linked, static documents held on servers distributed across the Internet" (p. 214). However, the web began to evolve and gradually started to harness the "collective intelligence" of its users (p. 219). In this way, websites such as Amazon, e-bay, Flickr, Facebook, YouTube, and Wikipedia all rely on their users engaging with, creating, and editing content. An increasing

DOI: 10.1057/9781137413758.0004

interaction with users was acknowledged around the year 2004, leading to the naming of this iteration of the web as Web 2.0, in direct contrast to the previous iteration of the web (Web 1.0) which was traditionally a one-way, read-only medium (pp. 220–1).

According to Levene (2010), the web "is undoubtedly the largest information repository known to man" (p. 10) and, as stated earlier, the web is particularly attractive to linguists precisely because of its size. However, providing a definitive answer to its actual size is not easy. Fletcher (2007) explains that "the web is constantly changing and growing and even the best estimates can only approximate its extent and composition" (p. 25). Nonetheless, several attempts have been made to estimate the size of the web. Levene (2010) summarises the results and reports that in 1993 there were only 130 publicly accessible websites but by 1998, there were approximately 320 million web pages and around 800 million in 1999. In July 2000 the web was estimated to consist of 2.1 billion pages (pp. 10–4). Fletcher (2007) reports that in 2005, the size of the web was estimated in the range between 10 and 20 billion web pages (p. 25), whilst the estimate for the beginning of 2010 stands at approximately 21 billion pages (Levene, 2010: 12). Naughton (2012) reports 2011 estimates somewhere in the range of 20 and 40 billion (p. 58) whilst in 2013, it was reported that there were 30 trillion unique web pages (Koetsier, 2013). Even though these are estimates, the web has unarguably grown exponentially from just a few hundred pages to many billion, if not trillion.

In terms of users, in June 2012, an estimated 2,405,518,376 people accessed the internet (representing approximately 34% of the world's population), compared to 360,985,492 users in December 2000 (Miniwatts Marketing Group, 2014). More up-to-date figures of both the number of web pages and users for the period in which this is written (mid-2014) do not appear to be available. However, the totals presented are sufficient for making the following point: given the extent to which these users interact – writing blogs, submitting customer reviews, updating social networking sites, and so on – it is clear to see why the web is considered by many to be such a powerful linguistic resource. In 2004, Coulthard explained that the metaphor of linguistic fingerprints in forensic authorship attribution is misleading "because it leads us to imagine the creation of massive databanks consisting of representative linguistic samples (or summary analyses) of millions of idiolects, against which a given text could be matched and tested. In fact such an enterprise is, and for the foreseeable future will continue to be, impractical if not impossible" (p. 432). A decade later this is still true, but taking into account the size of the web and the number of users, perhaps such an enterprise is no longer as impractical and impossible as it once seemed.

2.2   The nature of search engines

The typical way to search the web is through a search engine, which Fielden and Kuntz (2002) describe as:

> [N]othing more than automated software that matches a searcher's topic terms (keywords) with an indexed list of documents found on the Web or in some other collection, arranges that list according to some order of relevancy, and provides hyperlinks to those documents so that they may be visited. (p. 13, *original emphasis removed*)

As such, it is necessary to engage – albeit at a less than technical level – with how search engines operate, along with a consideration of their limitations, particularly from a linguist's perspective.

According to Fielden and Kuntz (2002), the search query itself is what most people associate with a search engine and they suggest – whimsically – that a search query works in the following manner:

> You call up the URL of your favoured search engine, type your topic words into the handy little text-box the search engine provides, press the "search" button and the little monster of a search engine goes off and brings back a list of items for your perusal. (p. 29)

In other words, individual lexical items and/or strings are entered into the search engine, at which point the "search engine then engages in a matching game" (p. 29).

Search engines have, working behind the scenes, a series of "web crawlers" (or "robots") – computer programs – which visit and store in databases as many web pages as they can by following the various links contained in those pages. The web crawlers therefore keep finding and collecting pages until they hit a dead end. As part of this process, the web pages are passed to an "indexer" – software which produces an index of the lexical content found in each page. When a user types a search query into a search engine, it is this index which is used to find web pages that match the user's query. Although the technology differs, this is not dissimilar to a reader consulting the index of a book in order to find a relevant page for a specific topic of interest. Where the analogy

DOI: 10.1057/9781137413758.0004

ends, of course, is that the index in a book remains static whereas the web does not. It is therefore not sufficient for search engines to crawl the web only once and as a consequence, "search engines are involved in an uphill struggle to cover as much of the Web as they can" (Levene, 2010: 82). Ntoulas, Cho and Olston (2004) highlight that because some web pages are regularly revised and updated, others are deleted, and news ones are created, indexes that are not kept up-to-date will become obsolete. Furthermore, search engines usually have multiple copies of their indexes stored on different servers, so as a consequence of the updating process, some servers have access to older versions of indexes than others. Search results therefore "will vary depending on the servers from which results are retrieved" (Levene, 2010: 81). Overall, coverage of the web is essential for search engines in order to ensure that they offer both quality and relevance (Levene, 2010: 82) and the consequence of an obsolete or outdated database is that a searcher can be led to irrelevant pages, or pages that no longer exist.

To gain a sense of how the sizes of indexes vary between search engines, in early 2004, Google was reported to have an index based on a database of 4.28 billion web pages, which had doubled to eight billion by the end of the year. MSN Search had an index based on over five billion pages in 2004, as did Yahoo! search, whilst Ask Jeeves reported an index of over two billion pages (Levene, 2010: 11). These figures compare with older estimates of search engine indexes, which were roughly between one and three billion for various search engines in 2002 (p. 11). This serves to highlight that not only does the web grow, but so too does the technology that enables searches of the web, and, crucially, indexes grow at different rates depending on the search engine used.

Fielden and Kuntz (2002) warn that no web search "ever encompasses the totality of the beast" (p. 18). Given that web crawlers could, pending resources, theoretically crawl the entire web, the question of why they do not must be asked since, as Schäfer and Bildhauer (2013) also claim, "exhaustive crawls are practically impossible" (p. 15). The answer lies in the fact that search engines simply do not have access to the entire web.

Despite the web size estimates provided in Section 2.1, the reality is that only a small fraction of this is actually indexable, that is, discoverable by web crawlers. A distinction therefore exists between the "accessible" and the "hidden" (also known as the "deep" or "invisible") web. Fletcher (2007) comments that the estimated 10–20 billion web pages that were accessible at the time represented "only the tip of the iceberg"

DOI: 10.1057/9781137413758.0004

of the information available on the web (p. 25). Web pages that cannot be accessed by web crawlers – and therefore are not publicly accessible – include those that require login credentials to access the content (for instance social network sites, forums and message boards, and subscription services), and web pages that will only be served to recognised and authorised IP addresses – for instance, company intranet pages. Other web sites only serve content after a form or questionnaire has been completed. Furthermore, some web pages which would otherwise be publicly accessible evade the web crawlers by including an exclusion file in the root directory which tells the web crawlers whether they are allowed to index the web pages. Schäfer and Bildhauer (2013) explain that web pages falling into this latter category are not technically classed as the hidden web, but, in terms of using the web as a corpus, they are nonetheless inaccessible (p. 10). According to Levene (2010), the size of the hidden web is estimated to be 550 times larger than the indexable web (p. 10), and Naughton (2012) reports estimates of the hidden web being between 400 and 750 times larger than the accessible web (p. 58).

The fact that search engines strive for providing quality and relevance for the people who use their search engines is motivated by the fact that they are commercial entities, driven by commercial interests, which also has ramifications for searching the web. As Rayson, Charles and Auty (2012) explain, search engines aim to return " 'useful' results to consumers, in the shortest time possible" (p. 23). Clearly, the better the results to the search query, the more users will turn to a particular search engine for their search queries, giving the search engines more opportunity to exploit commercial opportunities such as selling advertising space, or as Fletcher (2007) explains:

> Commerce drives today's web, with significant consequences for online linguistic research. The large general-purpose search sites we must rely on are business ventures, developed and operated at enormous expense. They provide essential services in exchange for advertising fees, and "paid positioning" is intended to steer searchers away from more relevant "natural" search results toward advertisers' sites. (p. 30)

Indeed, the fact that search engines are commercially driven means that they are susceptible to the same economic concerns as other enterprises, namely that they can go through periods of growth and reduction. This is highlighted by Rayson, Charles and Auty (2012) who explain that five years, in web terms, is a long time when it comes to change. For instance, Google has continued to grow, Yahoo! has undergone radical changes,

DOI: 10.1057/9781137413758.0004

and AltaVista, which had previously dominated the search engine market, no longer enjoys this success. Likewise, new competitors (such as Microsoft's Bing, formally Live) have entered the market (p. 23).

Given this commercial focus, the developers of search engines carry out optimisation procedures so that they provide the most relevant information and therefore attract and retain new users. A range of techniques are used in this regard. The first is that as much information as possible is indexed from web pages, including strings of numbers and characters since these are often bar codes, catalogue numbers, telephone numbers, and the like which might be useful for e-shopping (Levene, 2010: 95). Secondly, some words occur so frequently in documents that their utility in search queries becomes redundant. Therefore, when devising search queries, it is important to consider that most search engines will discard stopwords, which typically include articles, prepositions, many verbs, and frequently adverbs and adjectives (Fielden & Kuntz, 2002: 51). Therefore, search queries comprising the articles *a*, *an*, and *the* will not make good searches, and nouns "are almost always the best" (p. 51).

A third technique used for optimising search queries is stemming. This technique removes the suffixes of words in the index so that only the root form is indexed (Levene, 2010: 95). This is more efficient since a single root such as *telephon* can be indexed which will match the variant forms *telephone, telephoned, telephones, telephoning, telephony*, and so on in a user's search query, without having to store all of the separate forms in the index, leading to more refined indexes. Levene (2010) also explains that indexers typically convert all words to lower case, since this again reduces the size of the index (p. 96). Indexers therefore do not typically distinguish between *polish* and *Polish*, *lima* and *Lima*, *august* and *August*, and so on.

A further technique for search optimisation is related to the number of search results which are returned for search queries. For instance, typing the search query *linguistics* into the Google search engine produces 11,600,000 results at the time of writing. Rayson, Charles and Auty (2012) highlight that the total number of search results is actually an estimation – certainly for the larger commercial search engines – rather than an exact figure. Furthermore, these estimates are based on a combination of factors which are typically trademarked and not public knowledge (p. 23), and Kilgarriff and Grefenstette (2003) explain that the frequencies given for a simple search (e.g. the number of pages containing *x*) can vary dramatically, depending on how much load is placed on

DOI: 10.1057/9781137413758.0004

a particular search engine at any one time. Furthermore, search engines do not always provide the full extent of instances (p. 345). On this point, Schäfer and Bildhauer (2013) argue that since the designers of search engines focus on the precision of relevance, rather than the number of results that they can find, "we can never be sure that we have found all or even some of the linguistically relevant results" (p. 2). This is especially significant since the number of matching search results is a figure often used by linguists when there are no attested examples of words or phrases in existing corpora (Rayson, Charles & Auty, 2012: 24). For the forensic linguist, such a statistic can be used to determine the distinctiveness, or idiolectal potential, of a word or phrase (e.g. Coulthard, 2004).

Still on the issue of the number of matching search results, the counts that are produced are based on whichever documents have been deemed worthy of inclusion – based on criteria that are not publicly available – in the search engine's index. However, such counts are typically page counts rather than token counts (Schäfer & Bildhauer, 2013: 2). To return to the example provided earlier, the Google search query for *linguistics* identified 11,600,000 matching web pages, but this figure likely represents the number of pages containing *linguistics*, rather than the number of times that *linguistics* actually occurs on the web pages in its database. The number of matches therefore provides "only a general indication" of the frequency of a word or phrase and "these numbers cannot prove the prevalence of appropriateness of a given formulation" (Fletcher, 2007: 36). This situation is further compounded by the fact that not all of the text on web pages is actually indexed, with Fletcher (2007) reporting that only the first 100,000 words are indexed (p. 37). Overall then, taking into account how they are generated and the factors that affect them, frequency counts are subject to a great deal of distortion (Lüdeling, Evert and Baroni, 2007: 14).

Schäfer and Bildhauer (2013) highlight some additional areas where search queries are optimised. They highlight that the ranking criteria used by search engines to determine the order in which search results are shown, and particularly those that appear close to the top of the list, are unknown but are likely to include an element of sponsored ranking – that is, where the owners of web pages pay the search engine companies in order to get their pages to the top of the lists. Meta-data within the browser also affects search results. Notably, the user's language and geographical location influences which results are displayed so that results which are more geographically relevant are provided. For instance, searching simply for *supermarkets* in Google brings up a list of the super-market branches that appear to be closest in terms of proximity.

In a further effort to improve efficiency and precision, search engines also modify the user's search query. This includes correcting spelling, relying on the stemming techniques mentioned above, and analysing query logs (information about all of the queries submitted by searchers which are specific to each search engine) in order to improve the search query by anticipating what the searcher actually wanted to find, rather than what they typed into the search engine. In this regard, it is never fully known to the user what actual search has been performed. Additionally, because the web was not designed as a corpus or by linguists, searches cannot be specified in accordance with linguistic criteria, such as word class or citation form (Kilgarriff & Grefenstette, 2003: 345), although it should be noted that this is changing with development of software such as WebCorp, which allows for this provision – notably though, WebCorp is essentially a gateway to search engines and so is still subject to the more general fallacies and limitations of using search engines directly to access the web for linguistic research (Lüdeling, Evert & Baroni, 2007: 16).

At this juncture, a potential defence for using search engine query results in linguistics research may be that search results can, to some extent, be filtered. Lüdeling, Evert & Baroni (2007) describe four filters that can be applied: (i) language filters which specify which languages to search amongst for results; (ii) domain names (e.g. *.com, .co.uk*) which could be assumed to be used to approximate geographic region but actually such a filter is "extremely unreliable" (p. 15); (iii) file format (e.g. HTML, .pdf., .docx, .ppt) although Lüdeling, Evert and Baroni suggest this is less likely to be relevant to the majority of linguistics studies; and (iv) date filters for specifying whether to search web pages that have been updated in the last three, six, or 12 months (p. 15). Of course, such filters do not mitigate or otherwise compensate the problems with using search engines outlined earlier.

In summary, according to Schäfer and Bildhauer (2013), the search tools that would usually be used in dedicated corpus linguistics software such as *WordSmith Tools* (e.g. wildcarding for parts of speech tags) are not available and there is no way to be sure that all examples of the feature under investigation have been identified when using a search engine. In this way, then, "search engine query results are not uniform random samples from the search engine's index, but the exact opposite, namely samples which are extremely biased towards documents which

DOI: 10.1057/9781137413758.0004

the search engine provider has classified as relevant according to some metric unknown to the user" (p. 17).

Just as the web has evolved and developed (see Section 2.1), so too have search engines. Fletcher (2007) describes three developments in particular, with early search engines (c.1997) relying on information on the web page and being appropriate for full-text searches and lexical string matching which was suitable for seeking information from the web (p. 30). Following this, around 1998, information derived "off-page" – information about the quality of the page such as Google's PageRank metric which decides how important a web page is by considering how many other web pages are linked to it (Ntoulas, Cho & Olston, 2004: 6) – enabled effective searching for both information-seeking and web navigation queries. Then, moving into the early 2000s, developers of search engines started to focus their attention on understanding why users were carrying out their searches; in other words, developing systems to "identify the 'need behind the query' to identify relevant results – while providing targeted advertising" (p. 30). That search engines have themselves evolved in terms of how they produce results perhaps adds a confounding issue – not only is the web not static, but so too are search engines susceptible to changing practices and algorithms which further raises the need to establish the reliability of searching the web for forensic evidence.

2.3   The reliability of search engines

With this understanding of how search engines operate, it is reasonable to question just how reliable results obtained through searching the web actually are and on this point Levene (2010) is unequivocal:

> If we pose the same query to two search engines we will inevitably get different answers, and as search engine indexes are constantly changing, and they are continuously finding ways to improve their results, posing the same query to the same search engine will most likely give different results within relatively short time intervals. (p. 20)

Lüdeling, Evert and Baroni (2007) make the same point when they argue that unlike experiments carried out using traditional corpora, since "the web is constantly in flux" (p. 11), using the web as a corpus (see Section 2.4) means "it is impossible to replicate an experiment in an exact way at a later time" (p. 11).

DOI: 10.1057/9781137413758.0004

Two pieces of research in particular have set out to test the reliability of results generated from web searches, each of which will now be discussed. In the first, Blair, Urland and Ma (2002) designed an experiment which set out to examine whether search engines provide valid and reliable estimates of word frequencies since "the fluid nature of the Internet may undermine the reliability of estimates based on Internet databases" (p. 287). Search queries were based on 382 words, 250 of which were standard English nouns, verbs, and adjectives, whilst the remaining 132 non-standard words comprised 36 slang terms and 96 forenames, and were entered into four popular search engines: AltaVista, Northern Light, Excite, and Yahoo! According to Blair, Urland and Ma (2002), at the time when they carried out their research AltaVista and Northern Light had relatively large databases of over 200 million web pages, whilst Yahoo! had a database of approximately 150 million web pages and Excite contained just two million. They also explained that Yahoo! searched in a different way to the other three search engines, looking for general topics in its subject directory rather than keyword matching. To assess validity, the results from the search engine queries were compared to word frequencies obtained from Kučera and Francis' *Computational Analysis of Present-Day American English*, published in 1967, the CELEX linguistic database (an electronic database comprising 160,594 words from 284 written texts), and participant ratings of familiarity, in which 33 undergraduate students rated each word on a five-point scale, considering how frequently they had encountered the words, or how well they knew the words (p. 287).

They found that the differences in size between the search engine databases meant that the two larger search engines provided significantly higher estimates of word frequency than the two smaller search engines, and furthermore that all four search engines provided higher word estimates than obtained from the *Computational Analysis of Present-Day American English* and CELEX linguistic database. However, more important was the validity and reliability of the word frequency estimates, which was calculated through correlations of the word frequency estimates among the sources. They found that the search engine estimates were highly correlated with the *Computational Analysis of Present-Day American English* and CELEX linguistic database, but that the search engine estimates were only moderately correlated with participants' ratings (p. 288). Furthermore, the four search engines under investigation "provided highly consistent estimates of word frequency" (p. 288) amongst each other, and, when the analyses were repeated six months later, the search engines "produced highly reliable estimates over the 6-month period of time" (p. 288). These results led Blair, Urland and Ma to conclude that "Internet search engines provide word frequency estimates that are both valid and reliable" (p. 289). They did, however, advise researchers "to use search engines with large databases... to ensure the greatest representativeness" (p. 286), cautioning that the two smaller search engines in their study provided somewhat less accurate results (p. 290). Also, "with only a rough estimate of the total database (approximately 250 million) and the fact that it is always changing, the absolute frequencies of those words cannot be determined with any certainty" (p. 290).

Whilst their conclusion that search results are reliable is encouraging, several questions must be asked. Firstly, whilst repeating their research six months later proved to be fruitful, can the same be said of analysis carried out at a later interval, in other words, can reliability be maintained over a longer period of time? Lüdeling, Evert and Baroni (2007) explain that simply repeating web searches a few months after the original searches is a flawed approach. They explain that whilst some researchers claim that gaining similar results from repeated searches demonstrates reliability, what they have actually done is made a mistake whereby "they have succumbed to the statistical fallacy of using a non-independent data set for validation" (p. 12). Lüdeling, Evert and Baroni argue that a search engine's database changes over even a short period of time but repeating the searches at the second point in time "will still contain almost all the web pages from the first one, except for those that were modified or deleted in the meantime" (p. 12). As such, a drastic change in search results across two periods of time should not be expected. The exception is when the search query is restricted to pages which have been only recently added to the index, for instance, searching for neologisms that have arisen in the interval(s) between the first and repeated searches. In fact, Lüdeling, Evert and Baroni argue that if substantial differences in search query results are found across different periods of time, this is likely to be attributable to changes in indexing and different implementations of search technology (p. 12). Ntoulas, Cho and Olston (2004), based on an analysis of 154 websites (equivalent to an average of 4.4 million web pages) over a 51-week period between October 2002 and 2003, estimated that only 20 per cent of the web pages available at one point in time would be available one year later. If this is true, this calls into question how reliable search engine results are for periods of longer than one year.

DOI: 10.1057/9781137413758.0004

Further issues arising from Blair, Urland and Ma (2002) centre around their caution that researchers should use search engines with the larger databases, but quite whether it is possible to know the optimum size of a database for forensic linguistics research is questionable, not least because the size of the web keeps changing. It should also be borne in mind that, as explained in Section 2.2, word frequency results – fundamental to Blair, Urland and Ma's research – are based on estimations, and, more importantly, based on the number of pages containing the word, rather than the total numbers of words.

In a second study published a decade later, Rayson, Charles and Auty (2012) set out to investigate the reliability of search engine word counts with far more data, and over longer periods of time than previous studies, due to the lack of "any concrete information on how to best attain search result counts, and be sure of the accuracy" (p. 24). They expected that the search engines under investigation (Google, Yahoo! and Bing) estimated result counts because of the commercial requirement for speed (as outlined in Section 2.2), and that furthermore, results change at different periods. They therefore predicted that when carrying out search queries, none of the search engines would agree on the result counts, and that result counts would fluctuate over time. However, they did hope that despite fluctuation, results would settle around a central value (which would increase as the search engine's index increases), and that estimates would trend in similar patterns.

To test these predictions, they carried out a series of experiments, two of which are directly relevant here. In the first experiment, the top 1,000 single words and a random selection of 2,000 multi-word expressions of between two and five words in length were selected from the British National Corpus (BNC). Using the 1,000 single words and 2,000 multi-word expressions, a total of 3,000 individual search queries were carried out using the Google, Yahoo!, and Bing search engines every six hours for 20 weeks, spanning October 2009 to March 2010. The results showed that Google was almost constantly stable in the results it returned, although there was a period of considerable instability for eight days in January 2010, where the word count increased by 15 per cent then dropped by eight per cent, which, according to Rayson, Charles and Auty (2012) illustrates "the unpredictable nature of search engines" (p. 25). Overall, Yahoo! was shown to be more stable than Google, although it too had a period of instability lasting for only three days, although at a different time to Google. Rayson, Charles and Auty explain that these periods of instability

DOI: 10.1057/9781137413758.0004

were likely "due to temporary system difficulties" (p. 25). On the other hand, Bing showed a great deal of instability in the first two months of the period under investigation, but then stabilised. As the youngest of the search engines (by between 12 and 14 years), Bing would likely have had "radically different indexes to Google and Yahoo!" (p. 25).

To exemplify the problems of relying on search engine word counts, a series of queries were highlighted for further discussion, including the multi-word expression *best of both worlds*. Rayson, Charles and Auty (2012) explain that this multi-word expression was fairly stable as a search query in Google, with search result counts changing little more than five per cent between days. They report that Yahoo! was even more stable with the exception of some variance on two occasions, whilst Bing fluctuated wildly – in some cases by as much as 35 per cent. On this point, they commented that "search engines do not commonly correlate as far as stability is concerned" (p. 26). Such fluctuations mean that results taken at one point of flux are not necessarily representative of results taken at another period of stability. Further discrepancy was highlighted by the actual frequencies reported by the search engines, with Bing returning 55 million results for the search query *best of both worlds*, Google returning 1.6 million, and Yahoo! returning just 320,000 results (p. 26). Over the period of time, fewer results were actually identified by Bing and Yahoo!, whilst the Google results remained stable.

In their second experiment, Rayson, Charles and Auty (2012) wanted to determine whether variability would be observed outside of the high-frequency words. They therefore selected ten high-frequency words and ten low-frequency words from the BNC, as well as the names of ten UK towns and cities. Yahoo! was not used for this experiment because, unlike during the first experiment, the programming interface required for automating the search queries was no longer free to use. The search queries were repeated every 12 hours for five weeks in 2011. For the ten high-frequency words, similar overall patterns were obtained, although they did note that the words *by* and *that* were ranked differently relative to the other words. More difference was detected between Google and Bing for the low-frequency words, with Bing's estimates being ten times higher than Google's. This led Rayson, Charles and Auty to conclude that their results "show conflicting trends and provide a strong hint that search result count estimates are calculated by very different mechanisms in Google and Bing" (p. 28). For the ten UK city and town place names, Bing again produced results that were around ten times higher than

DOI: 10.1057/9781137413758.0004

Google, but following the same overall trends. The names of five cities in particular, however, did produce radically different results, which Rayson, Charles and Auty suggest was possibly due to search optimisation – refining the search to take into account their geographical location.

Rayson, Charles and Auty's (2012) research highlights some interesting points which require further investigation if the web is to be used for forensic purposes. Firstly, they acknowledge instability in results from search engine queries – in fact, all three search engines investigated experienced periods of instability of differing lengths. One reasonable explanation for instability provided by Rayson, Charles and Auty is temporary technical problems with the systems. For general search queries this is unlikely to be problematic, but from a forensic perspective, linguists must question how much instability and technical difficulty they are willing to tolerate when producing evidence, and whether they would ever know that their queries have been affected by such instability. Given that all three search engines investigated were susceptible to instability, it is likely that this problem is more pervasive than perhaps was highlighted by Blair, Urland and Ma (2002).

Rayson, Charles and Auty (2012) also explain that variance between search engine results for different search engines may be because of the age of the search engine, and therefore the size of its database. This same point is made by Blair, Urland and Ma (2002). It seems then that for forensic linguists to use the web as evidence, they need to be satisfied that the search engine being used has a sufficiently large database; quite how a linguist can be sure of the optimum size of a database though is unclear, not least because the web is in a constant state of flux so the ratio of web size to database size will constantly vary. Essentially, the forensic linguist is required to use the biggest search engine out of the available choices and, as highlighted in Section 2.2, as commercial entities, the biggest search engines will likely be the ones that provide the most biased results.

It is also important to recognise from Rayson, Charles and Auty's (2012) research that different search engines provided different results. Using just the example of their multi-word string *best of both worlds* reveals that Bing reported 55 million matches, whilst Yahoo! matched only a mere 320,000 hits. If forensic linguists turn to the web as evidence regarding the distinctiveness of a word or phrase, then clearly different inferences can be drawn from such starkly different results. In this context, *best of both worlds* looks more distinctive when using Yahoo! than when searching for the same multi-word string using Bing – in itself a subjective claim since it is not possible to know exactly what was searched or what this number actually represents. However, Blair, Urland and Ma (2002) found that search engine results were consistent with each other, so what can account for these different conclusions? One possible explanation is that since both pieces of research were carried out over a decade apart, in the intervening period the web has exploded in size and search engines have developed algorithms for searching that are perhaps more advanced, secretive, and crucially different, than in 2002. It should also be noted that Blair, Urland and Ma (2002) repeated their analyses at a six-month interval, whereas Rayson, Charles and Auty (2012) repeated their search queries far more frequently and over a 12-month period, so any variance and instability would likely be more apparent in their study. If this is the case, it might be predicted that repeating searches in a short period of time (of less than six months) produces reliable results, but repeating the searches after a much longer period of time (of over one year), does not produce reliable results. The empirical work reported in Chapters 3 and 4 considers this question further.

Having considered what the web is, how it is searched, and some of the reliability issues incumbent with using search engines, it is now possible to consider the web not as a massive online source of information ready for searching, but as a corpus for linguistics research.

2.4   The web as corpus

When describing the web as a tool in corpus linguistics, a distinction is typically made between using the web *as* a corpus, and using the web *for* a corpus. In the first sense, the web itself is considered as the corpus to be consulted, which is searched using commercial search engines and subject to the problems raised in Section 2.2. In the second sense, the web is treated as "a source of machine-readable texts for corpus compilation" (Fletcher, 2007: 28) which can be selected and stored offline. In other words, this second sense refers to using the web for specialised corpus building (Hundt, Nesselhauf & Biewer, 2007: 2). Following the procedure related to the UNABOM trial as described by Coulthard (2000) in Chapter 1, the focus of this research is on the use of the web as corpus for producing evidence. Therefore, using the web for corpus construction will not receive further attention here (cf. Schäfer & Bildhauer, 2013, for an excellent introduction).

DOI: 10.1057/9781137413758.0004

McEnery and Wilson (1996) define corpus linguistics as "the study of language based on examples of 'real life' language use" (p. 1) and define a corpus in the following way: "In principle, any collection of more than one text can be called a corpus: the term 'corpus' is simply the Latin for 'body', hence a corpus may be defined as any body of text" (p. 21). Missing from this definition, however, is any reference to the purposes for data collection. Sinclair (1991) on the other hand defines a corpus as "a collection of naturally-occurring language text, *chosen* to character-ize a state or variety of a language" (p. 171, *my emphasis*). The definition is not entirely dissimilar from that of McEnery and Wilson (1996), yet the inclusion of *chosen* implies that there must be a purpose behind the data collection and that the data must be selected in accordance with this purpose. Therefore, by consequence, a corpus is perhaps not simply just a collection of more than one text, but rather a collection of texts, each of which has been specifically chosen in order to "characterize a state or variety of a language" (Sinclair, 1991: 171). The issue of size is illustrated by Leech (1991) who defines a corpus as "a sufficiently large body of naturally occurring data of the language to be investigated" (p. 8). However, in the forensic context, building sufficiently large corpora is not always possible and as Shuy (2002) suggests, "one works with what one has" (p. 355). Coulthard (1994) recommends that forensic linguists should compare QDs with a "small and case-specific corpus gathered for comparative purposes" (p. 30) and since the problem of size cannot always readily be solved, attention tends to focus on representativeness.

Lindquist and Levin (2000) argue that representativeness should be the major concern when selecting or constructing a corpus and Kilgarriff and Grefenstette (2003) argue that whilst the web is big, a common retaliation to those who use it as a corpus is that it is not representative (p. 340). They suggest that rather than looking at representativeness, the milder term *balanced* should instead be used. They also argue that although the web is not representative of anything else, other than what it is, neither are other corpora (p. 343). On this point, Blair, Urland and Ma (2002) highlight that anyone can post to the web and so consequently, it may prove to be representative of "everyone's language" (p. 287). However, Leech (2007) cautions that claims of representativeness need to be substantiated and without such verification, the findings derived from a corpus cannot be accepted, and that "[w]ithout representativeness, whatever is found to be true of a corpus, is simply true of that corpus – and cannot be extended to anything else" (p. 135). With reference specifically to the web, Leech (2007)

DOI: 10.1057/9781137413758.0004

argues the web cannot be seen as representative of the English language, nor even of only written English language use since despite containing a wealth of different written genres (e.g. academic writing, fiction writing, personal narratives), and indeed a wealth of new and evolving genres (e.g. blogs and wikis), other areas are not represented to any great extent, if at all (e.g. private discourse including everyday conversation, telephone conversations). Leech argues that the "web in English is its own textual universe, with huge overlaps with the non-electronic textual universe of the English language. It is a textual universe of unfathomed extent and variety, but it can in no way be considered a representative sample of language use in general" (pp. 144–5).

Hunston (2002) claims that when considering representativeness, it is not uncommon to overlook "the diachronic aspect", whereby she warns that a "corpus that is not regularly updated becomes unrepresentative" (p. 30). Because the web is added to with such rapidity, it is unlikely to become diachronic. Leech (2007) adds that a further barrier to viewing the web as a diachronic corpus comes from the fact that it is not possible to know when texts were written and, nor too can the web be comfortably viewed as a synchronic corpus since only minimal information about the provenance of texts is available (p. 145). This invites the question of how the web as a corpus can be characterised. Hunston (2002) suggests that a general corpus is a "corpus of texts of many types" (p. 14). She further argues that such corpora can include written and/or spoken language and additionally that they can be produced in one or many countries. The result is that they are unlikely to be representative although they can be useful as a baseline for comparisons with specialised corpora (pp. 14–15). When considering the web as a corpus, it successfully fulfils each of these criteria in that it contains many different text types including written language and hybrid forms of spoken and written communication such as e-mail and chat room dialogue, produced all over the world, although, as Leech (2007) argues, spoken language is unlikely to be represented. Alternatively, the specialised corpus only contains texts of a particular type, with the aim of being representative only of a given type of text (Hunston, 2002) and whilst the web as a whole cannot therefore be considered to be a specialised corpus, specific areas of the web can perhaps be used as specialised sub-corpora. For example, if a corpus of academic English was required, it would be possible to consult an online, academic English journal, or if medical language was required, it would be possible to consult an online

DOI: 10.1057/9781137413758.0004

medical journal – although of course these are mainly digitised versions of books rather than sub-corpora which are unique to the web.

Monitor corpora are added to at regular intervals so that their size increases rapidly. In this respect, the web can be viewed as a monitor corpus as information is constantly being added at a rate far faster than could ever be calculated. However, the main difference between the web and a monitor corpus is in the design. Hunston (2002) claims that a monitor corpus is designed to track current changes in a language and that additionally, "the proportion of text types in the corpus remains constant, so that each year (or month or day) is directly comparable with every other" (p. 16), and here, clearly the web does not have the same restrictions imposed upon it. However, Sinclair (1991) argues that monitor corpora have no end date, because like language, they keep on developing (p. 25) and the web is certainly similar in this respect; however, the web was not designed to track language development, which Hunston (2002) explains is a requirement of monitor corpora, making it difficult to fully characterise the web as corpus in this way.

An easier label to apply is that of the "raw corpus" (Hänlein, 1999: 79) since web pages are not typically annotated or tagged. Whilst the lack of tagging and annotation is problematic for many types of corpus analysis, Čermák (2002) sees the raw nature of any corpus as positive, arguing that the best information comes directly from data in its "pure unadulterated" form because annotated data is biased (p. 279). Such bias can arise through part-of-speech tagging which can be subjective due to different levels of accuracy in transcription and tagging (Lindquist & Levin, 2000). It therefore appears that whilst the web may share features with several different types of corpora, it may best be described as a raw, general corpus.

2.5 Searching the web to produce forensic linguistics evidence

At this juncture, it is worthwhile questioning how the information presented in this chapter relates to linguistics research, and more specifically, to linguistics evidence produced to assist with the pursuit of justice in the criminal justice system. Therefore, taking into account the issues so far discussed, this chapter concludes by considering the issues specifically from the perspective of a forensic linguist.

DOI: 10.1057/9781137413758.0004

Schäfer and Bildhauer (2013) argue that for all of the reasons outlined in Section 2.2, the practice of drawing statistical inference from search query result counts must "be considered bad science by any account" (p. 2). In short, summarising Schäfer and Bildhauer (2013: 2–3) and Section 2.2, linguistic evidence derived from using web search engines is subject to the following fallacies:

i   Search engines are programmed to provide quality of results rather than quantity; linguists therefore have no way to be sure that all instances of a search term have been found;

ii Results are ranked and displayed according to criteria which are not widely known, but for which paid advertising is likely to be a big factor; this may not necessarily be problematic other than any attestations of a word or phrase found using a search engine will not have been randomly sampled;

iii Meta-data such as the searcher's preferred language and location influence results so that two identical searches will almost never return the same results; reliability cannot therefore be demonstrated, which Schäfer and Bildhauer (2013) argue is "a clear indication of bad science" (p. 2);

iv Search queries are automatically optimised by the search engine – including correcting spellings and stemming amongst others – all based on the analysis of search engine query logs. It is therefore not possible to know exactly what the result counts from a search actually represent (i.e. the results displayed do not necessarily match what was typed into the search engine). Peer-reviewed journals would be unlikely to publish research where corpus statistics are cited but the search node is never revealed. Whether such data should be used in forensic investigations is therefore questionable;

v   The number of results obtained from search queries is only an estimate and since it is not possible to know what the estimates are based on or how accurate they are, forensic linguists are required to put all of their faith in whatever statistic the search engine provides;

vi The results obtained from search queries are typically page counts and not token counts and so the forensic linguist who infers that word or phrase x is more or less frequent than y is making an assumption about how balanced the web is and that neither x nor y have been over- or under-represented on a particular web page;

DOI: 10.1057/9781137413758.0004

vii There is no way to know what has, or what has not, been included
     in the search engine's index, nor which parts of the web have been
     indexed so the forensic linguist is at the mercy of whatever index
     was most commercially viable; and
viii Search engine's indexes are constantly updated and change
     frequently. Again, results cannot be replicated which leads Schäfer
     and Bildhauer (2013) to conclude rather damningly that "[e]ven
     if all other points of criticism put forward here were invalid, this
     single fact makes reporting search engine results bad science" (p. 3).
     The legal system is no place for bad science.

Taking into account these criticisms of using the web as a corpus, it seems
that at best, search engines have the potential for some unreliability,
whilst at worst they might be considered a form of bad science leading
to results which are biased in favour of commercial interests – a form
of contaminated data. On this point, Eder (2013) offers the following
analogy: "[r]elying on contaminated data is similar to using dirty test
tubs in a laboratory: it inescapably means falling into systematic error"
(p. 604). Fletcher (2007) argues that "evidence for any claim or conclusion
must be subject to inspection and alternate analysis by other researchers" (p. 37) and for forensic linguists, where the stakes of using evidence
about language is arguably higher than linguistics research since liberty
may be at stake, replication, inspection, and scrutiny of both data and
results by others is fundamental – the cornerstone of the adversarial
legal system, perhaps. Rosenbach (2007) argues that not knowing where
web data actually comes from, coupled with the "ever shifting nature of
the data pool", all leads to analysis which is "basically non-replicable"
(p. 168). Fletcher (2007) explains that in a best case scenario, "the laws of
large numbers permit *comparable* results for frequent search terms, but
the composition of the actual web pages matched can be quite different"
(p.37, *original emphasis*). It appears then, that caution certainly needs to
be exercised when using data derived from the web, particularly word
frequency counts, since such data appears to be more prone to contami-
nation of results than is tolerable in a forensic context.

This creates something of a problem for the forensic linguist. On the
one hand, if web searches conducted using commercial search engines
can at least be shown to be reliable, as Rayson, Charles and Auty (2012)
and Blair, Urland and Ma (2002) argue, then perhaps linguistic evidence
can be obtained from the web, despite some of the other shortcomings.

DOI: 10.1057/9781137413758.0004

However, if reliability of the web is low, or if the methodological limitations of searching the web using commercial search engines are accepted, then questions must be asked about whether evidence obtained from the web is acceptable for use in forensic investigations. In the following two chapters, empirical research is described which begins to assess the reliability of web data for cases of authorship analysis.

DOI: 10.1057/9781137413758.0004

3

Attributing Documents to Unknown Authors Using Idiolectal Co-selection and the Web

Abstract: *In order to determine the extent to which idiolectal co-selection can be used as a marker of authorship, and the reliability of the web in producing such evidence, this chapter describes empirical research. Two documents are analysed in a scenario where no candidate authors are available for comparison. Core words, derivatives of core words, and subject-specific words are removed from the texts, leaving behind a set of potential idiolectal co-selections. The web is searched to determine the distinctiveness of these idiolectal co-selections, with analysis repeated seven days and ten years later in order to assess reliability. Results show that whilst targeted searches were successful to some extent, the results varied considerably over the ten-year period.*

Keywords: *authorship analysis; idiolectal co-selection; lexis; marker of authorship; reliability of web; reliability of search engines*

Larner, Samuel. *Forensic Authorship Analysis and the World Wide Web*. Basingstoke: Palgrave Macmillan, 2014. DOI: 10.1057/9781137413758.0005.

This chapter investigates whether, using idiolectal co-selection as a marker of authorship, evidence of authorship can be obtained from the web in a scenario where the linguist is presented with a QD and no KDs written by candidate authors. As explained in Chapter 1, Section 1.3, it is argued here that evidence of idiolectal co-selection as a marker of authorship will be stronger and more convincing if other documents written by the author of the QD are identified from web searches, since this will demonstrate that a group of words are used in a consistent fashion by an author across different texts. Clearly, if fewer other authors use the same group of words, then the argument that such idiolectal co-selections are distinctive to the author of the QD may be possible. If, on the other hand, considerably more other authors also use the same set of idiolectal co-selections, then the argument that they stand as a good marker of authorship is diminished. The following chapter then investigates whether a QD can be successfully attributed in this way when compared to texts produced by candidate authors.

According to Coulthard (2000), as explained in Chapter 1, during the UNABOM trial Lakoff singled out 12 lexical items and phrases which could be expected to occur in any text which argued a position. No information is provided about how these 12 lexical items and phrases were selected, but clearly a principled and replicable approach will need to be developed in order to assess the powerfulness of idiolectal co-selection as a marker of authorship, and indeed the viability of using the web in cases of authorship analysis. As such, the method outlined in this research is novel and all conclusions will necessarily be confined to this one approach. This point will be returned to in Chapter 5, Section 5.2.

3.1   Data and method

In order to investigate the extent to which the web can be used to assess the distinctiveness of idiolectal co-selection, data in the form of published articles whose authorship could be attested was selected. Since this chapter is concerned with attributing a QD when no suspects are available, only one document was required (QD1), and for this purpose, a linguistics article by Shuy (2002) was selected. This article was selected because it was readily available in electronic form from academic databases and did not require any manual inputting, where error could potentially be introduced. A second document (QD2) was also analysed – the

DOI: 10.1057/9781137413758.0005

Unabomber's terrorist manifesto – so that comparisons could be drawn between the findings of this research and that of the evidence produced during the UNABOM trial, as reported by Coulthard (2000). Again, the manifesto was available in electronic form and was downloaded from the web. Although QD1 is different from QD2 in respect of orientation, function, and even length, it was deemed important to select something different from the manifesto in order to begin to highlight any limitations of the method for identifying idiolectal co-selections that may arise. QD1 contained 5,858 words whilst QD2 was substantially longer, containing 34,581 words.

Sinclair (1991), when discussing the analysis of texts, comments that "[t]he safest policy is to keep the text as it is, unprocessed and clean of any other codes" (p. 21) because in this way, the subjectivity of the analyst is not imposed on the text. However, it was deemed necessary to process the QDs since they both contained direct quotation. Given that these were not the words used by each QD's author and were instead exact repetitions of other authors' words, they were deleted. On this point, Johnson (1997) chose to leave quotations in the original documents:

> It was the identical uncommon vocabulary which initially led me to link the three essays and to investigate further, although some of the uncommon vocabulary was found to be contained in quotations from published authors. However, the fact that identical quotations had been selected seemed to be a further link between the texts. (1997: 212)

However, it should be noted that Johnson was analysing documents for plagiarism and so could feasibly view shared quotations between documents as indicative of dual authorship. Because this research focuses on single-authored documents, the inclusion of direct quotations would potentially distort the author's idiolectal lexical choices. Quotations which were paraphrased were not deleted since these were assumed to represent each author's own linguistic choices. Proper nouns and numbers were also deleted since, due to the nature of the texts being academic in style, a high proportion of citation was present.[1]

A further consideration was punctuation. Computer analyses of text typically identify word-forms, which Sinclair (1991) describes as "an unbroken succession of letters" (p. 28). Sinclair further comments that the "computer can find, sort, and count word-forms fairly easily; it finds the conventional notion of a word much more vague and complicated, and there is not a standard procedure for converting word-forms to words" (p. 29). Sinclair

DOI: 10.1057/9781137413758.0005

explains that when considering the word-form as "an unbroken succession of letters", apostrophes and hyphens require special attention. The decision was therefore made to count word-forms which incorporated hyphens and apostrophes as separate word-forms. Therefore, *its* and *it's* were counted separately. Other punctuation marks (e.g. commas, colons, semi-colons, full stops, and parentheses) created several different word-forms where this would be less desirable since combining a word with different punctuation could lead to a variety of different word-forms for the same word. For instance, the word *ideally* occurring at the end of a sentence and combined with a full stop (*ideally.*) would be counted by the computer as a different word-form to the same word occurring before a comma (*ideally,*), before a semi-colon (*ideally;*), at the end of a question (*ideally?*), and so on. The decision was therefore made to remove punctuation from the QDs. Before this processing, QD1 contained 5,858 tokens whilst QD2 contained 34,581 tokens. After direction quotation, proper nouns, numbers, and punctuation were removed, QD1 was reduced to 4,997 tokens (1,391 types) whilst QD2 contained 33,436 tokens (4,045 types). As these totals show, QD2 is considerably larger than QD1, and likewise the ratio of types to tokens in QD2 is greater than that of QD1. Following this process, an alphabetical word list was created for each of the QDs which also included the total number of occurrences of each word.

Since the aim of this research is to establish a set of idiolectal co-selections which might be linked to an individual's authorial style, the decision was made to focus on distinctive lexis (this decision is given further consideration in Chapter 5, Section 5.2). To achieve this, the alphabetised word lists produced for each QD were refined by removing core vocabulary, derivatives of core vocabulary, subject-specific vocabulary, and shared vocabulary between the two QDs, each of which is now discussed in turn.

The concept of a core vocabulary is based on the notion that any speaker of a language will not know the entire vocabulary: "A large unabbreviated general dictionary such as the OED contains half a million entries, many of them unknown to most speakers. This gives us, in effect, a rough distinction between everyday and specialist words" (Stubbs, 1986: 104). Stubbs further argues that as part of a native speakers' linguistic competence, there is "the ability to recognize that some words are 'ordinary' English words, in some sense, whereas others are rare, exotic, foreign, specialist, regional and so on" (p. 101). Therefore, if these "ordinary" words, or core words, are removed from a text, the

DOI: 10.1057/9781137413758.0005

remaining lexical items could potentially be either topic related or more indicative of an individual author's idiolect. For example, Coulthard (1994) argues that the ten most frequent words represent 20% of a typical text, whilst the remaining 80% is comprised of the 2,500 most frequent words; consequently, the majority of English words are used infrequently (p. 28). Johnson (1997) assessed lexical overlap when detecting plagiarism, and found that when core vocabulary was excluded, texts shared only 6% of lexical items, which further suggests the potential for distinctive vocabulary use outside of the core vocabulary.

Although removing the core vocabulary from the word lists may be contentious, Love (2002) explains that a "clue to authorship is rare and unusual vocabulary" (p. 108) but also acknowledges that the real question is one of *how* rare and *how* unusual, and likewise Carter (1998) explains that "core vocabulary itself has no unambiguously clear boundaries" (p. 45). For the purposes of this research a core vocabulary list based on the 5,000 most frequent words in the Brown Corpus was compiled. The Brown Corpus was identified as the most suitable corpus given that both authors of the QDs were American authors. Carter (1998) explains that "[c]ore words will have to be words of high frequency but they will also need to have an evenness of range and coverage of texts in that broadest sense of the term"[2] (p. 46) and as the Brown Corpus contains different types of texts, to a limited extent, this was achieved. Francis and Kučera (1979) explain that the Brown Corpus consists of "1,014,312 words of running text of edited English prose printed in the United States during the calendar year of 1961" (p. 1) and, since it contains some documents which are journalistic in nature, and also some which are academic, it is potentially representative of the data used in this research. However, the frequency list was compiled in 1961, and so questions of representativeness pertaining to the date may be raised.[3]

In QD1, 947 lexical items were identified as core words and were subsequently removed (a small selection of examples include *accident, added, assigned, begun, belief, caught, classic, decision, develop,* and *education*), whilst in document QD2, 2,220 were removed from the document as core words (of which *amount, angry, artistic, basis, beautiful, careful, central, day, dealt,* and *eat* are all examples) leaving a list of 444 types for QD1 and 1,842 types for QD2. Of these core words, 696 were shared between both QD1 and QD2. Some examples of core words shared between the two QDs include *aside, average, avoid, building, business, create, crime, drawn, during,* and *effective.* From the original 5,000 word

DOI: 10.1057/9781137413758.0005

frequency list, 2,536 words did not occur in either document. It may therefore be questioned just how representative the list actually was; that is to say, whether it was a fair assumption to claim that the most frequent words were core words because if this was the case, more words should perhaps have been identified. As mentioned earlier, Johnson (1997) found that in the texts she was analysing, when core vocabulary was excluded, authors shared only 6% of lexical items. As she was investigating a case of suspected plagiarism, the texts she worked with were written on the same topic, in the same genre, and with shared direct quotation between them. Therefore, as QD1 and QD2 are unrelated in topic and direct quotation was removed, it would perhaps be expected that the shared vocabulary between QD1 and QD2 should be lower than 6%. In fact, 20 lexical items were shared between QD1 and QD2 which equated to 16% of the total lexis for QD1 being shared with QD2, but only 2.7% of the total lexical items for QD2, which provides two extremes and raises the question of whether a longer text was required for QD1, in order to provide a more satisfactory result.

As the process of removing core vocabulary did not remove as many words from the QD word lists as would have been expected, the decision was made to remove any word which was a derivative of a core word (e.g. *actively* was deemed to be a derivative of *active*, *aims* a derivative of *aim*, and *appealed* a derivative of *appeal*). Future studies may wish to revise this process due to its contentious nature, which is highlighted by Shuy (2002) when he argues that the past tense of *awake* (*awoke*) is rare in some dialects (p. 355). In QD1, 162 lexical items were identified as core derivatives, whilst in document QD2, 698 lexical items were excluded on this basis.

As should be expected, several of the words which remained in the word lists of QD1 and QD2 were particular to the topic of each document. It was decided that words which were subject-specific would be less likely to be indicative of authorial style in a text written about a different topic. They were therefore discarded and were, in the main, nouns that were independently judged to be subject-specific. In document QD1, 157 lexical items were identified as subject-specific (including *adjective, clause, crimes, dialectology, dialects, dictionaries, grammatically, lexicographers, linguistics,* and *noun*) and in document QD2, 371 lexical items were identified as such (e.g. *Aborigines, Afghanistan, anarchist, anthropologist, Australian, collectivism, diabetes, entomology, evangelists,* and *fascists*), leaving a word list containing 125 types for QD1 and 739 types for QD2.

DOI: 10.1057/9781137413758.0005

Following this refinement, the word lists for QD1 and QD2 were compared to each other in order to establish which lexical items (if any) were shared between the two documents on the assumption that any words which occurred between both documents could potentially be considered less distinctive. A total of 20 lexical items were shared between the two documents (e.g. *else, far, invaded, option, predict*), leaving QD1 with a type total of 105, and QD2 with a type total of 719. This left both QD1 and QD2 with word lists somewhat reduced from their original totals. Whilst high, 105 types for QD1 were considered to be a manageable quantity for analysis. However, 719 types for QD2 were considered to be too many to successfully determine the distinctiveness of each type using the web, and so an extra measure was required in order to reduce this total. Coulthard (2004) argues the "distinctiveness and diagnostic power of words used once-only" (p. 435) as indicative of authorship, particularly in plagiarism cases, with the opinion that two authors are less likely to use the same words only once in a document since, with such low frequency, these words are clearly not central to the topic being written about. Therefore, in an attempt to reduce the number of types in QD2, those words which occurred more than once were removed from the word list on the basis that hapax legomena may be particularly useful in determining authorship (e.g. Coulthard, 2004; Hoover, 2003). At the end of this phase, there remained a total of 497 types in QD2 (compared to 105 for QD1), which, whilst still a considerably high number, was deemed manageable. Since QD1 and QD2 were being analysed independently and were not being compared, it did not matter that there was a substantial difference between the sizes of the word lists for both documents.

Since the remaining words for each author of the QDs were not within the top 5,000 most frequent words (nor their derivatives), and were not specific to any one text or genre, and were not shared between each other, they could quite plausibly be distinctive and could be expected to occur in other texts produced by the same author whilst being less likely to be used by lots of other authors. For QD1, a sample of the remaining words includes *abundantly, array, everyday, incomplete, misleading, prevailed, simplicity, unforeseen, violates,* and *wreck,* whilst for QD2, a small sample includes *acutely, adopt, constraint, deficit, deserves, excludes, harsh, inclination, prudent,* and *unlimited.*

With a set of idiolectal co-selections identified for each of the authors of QD1 and QD2, it was then possible to assess each individual lexical

DOI: 10.1057/9781137413758.0005

item in the set for distinctiveness using the web. In other words, it was possible to determine the distinctiveness of each word, and then to determine whether any of the distinctive items were idiolectal co-selections. To assess this, two types of searches using the web were conducted: a targeted search in a restricted domain, and a more general search using commercial search engines.

3.2   Targeted searches

If each remaining word for each of the authors had been entered into a general search engine as a query, the amount of webpages returned would have been phenomenal, and therefore unmanageable. In the first instance then, it was necessary to conduct the searches of each individual word in a more targeted search. By placing restrictions upon the material to be searched, a more manageable number of results could be obtained, at which point it would be possible to determine the distinctiveness of the words and whether other authors appear to share the same combinations of words as the authors of QD1 and QD2. For QD1, the targeted searches were conducted on the same materials from which the source document was downloaded (*The Journal of American Speech*), accessed through the Ingenta Select academic database. At the time of searching (2004), the electronic version of this journal only contained articles published between the years 2000 and 2004, and as such, this was a particularly restricted search. Furthermore, given that the searches were carried out mid-2004, only two of the four volumes for that year had actually been published. The decision to search in this journal was motivated by representativeness in that all the authors who published in this journal were presumed to have a similar educational level as the author of QD1 and all texts searched would be of the same genre, namely academic articles. Each individual lexical item was entered into the *basic search* text box and the *include fulltext* option was checked, so that the search would consider all aspects of a document, and not, for example, just the title and abstract.

The search for QD2 author's lexical items was conducted in a similar manner. Kaczynski was prolific in the field of mathematics (Mello, 1999) and as such an initial search was conducted through the JSTOR database (a huge online database covering a massive range of articles published in many different academic journals). Kaczynski was specified as the author

DOI: 10.1057/9781137413758.0005

in only the mathematics journals (of which JSTOR had access to 15) and five documents were returned as authored by Kaczynski over the period of 1964 to 1969. On this basis, the targeted search was restricted to mathematics journals held in the JSTOR database, with only articles published between 1964 and 1969 being searched. Whilst this search looks very limited, a huge amount of data was actually being searched, although an estimate cannot be provided because it was impossible to determine how many articles from each journal were actually being searched. As with QD1, this search was deemed to be representative of the author of QD2 in terms of educational level even though the manifesto was known not to be published in this database. To begin the search, each lexical item was typed separately into the text box, and it was specified that the search engine should look in *fulltext*. The search was restricted to only mathematics journals, whilst the dates 1964 and 1969 were entered in the *Limit by Publication Date* area, to further restrict the search.

At the start of this chapter, it was predicted that, based on the set of lexical items derived from QD1, as a minimum the original QD should be identified from the targeted search, since this is from where it was originally downloaded. As predicted, for QD1 all 105 lexical items, entered separately, did include the source document in the search results. For example, the lexical item *variant* occurred in 42 documents, *everyday* in 29, and *candidly* in only one (which was QD1). Conducting this form of search allows further assumptions to be made about the distinctiveness of the lexis and how indicative it may be of authorship. From the examples above, it can be deduced that *variant*, due to its relatively high frequency in a refined search, is subject-specific (despite not having been identified as such at an earlier stage), or at least very common in this particular journal, making it of less use in establishing authorship. However, words such as *candidly, construe, exigencies*, and *imparting*, which occurred in only one document (QD1) appear to be especially distinctive. However, it cannot be surmised that they are useful predictors of authorship because they only occur in one document and could be chance occurrences of rare lexical items. Those lexical items of direct relevance therefore are those that occur in two or more documents authored by the same author, and of this group, only three lexical items produced such results: *confession, consult*, and *unintentionally*. All three lexical items occurred in two documents produced by QD1's author. However, it should also be noted that *confession* occurred in six documents in total, *consult* occurred in 11 documents, whilst *unintentionally*

DOI: 10.1057/9781137413758.0005

occurred in only two documents. Therefore, apart from *unintentionally*, we cannot claim that the author of QD1 is the only author to use these lexical items. However, it is precisely the combination of these three lexical items that appears to be idiolectal and distinctive, in that of all of the articles published in this database, only two contained a combination of all three lexical items, and both documents were authored by Shuy. Therefore, *confession, consult*, and *unintentionally*, for present purposes, appear to form a distinctive idiolectal co-selection for Shuy. Occurrences of these three lexical items were checked in both documents to ensure that they were used in different ways rather than, for example, instances of legitimate self-plagiarism across both documents. Additionally, it is interesting to note that whilst re-occurring words were not removed from QD1, the three lexical items discussed above were all hapaxes in QD1, which suggests that the decision to remove words which occurred more than once from QD2 was reasonable.

In order to assess reliability, this procedure was repeated a decade later. Access to the journal was this time provided by the academic database Project Muse, rather than Ingenta Select which was used in the original searches. Since the search was restricted to volumes of a specific journal published over a fixed period of time, the results should be exactly the same, since no new articles could have been published.[4] However, this was not the case. In fact, only 58 of the results for the words in this set of lexical items were the same in 2014 as they were in 2004, with 36 of the results increasing, and 11 decreasing. Both the increases and the decreases are unexpected since the search terms and the search parameters remained the same. A likely explanation is that the search algorithms used by Project Muse differ from those used by Ingenta Select, although this is difficult to verify. In order to triangulate results, the searches were repeated by searching *American Speech* directly from the Duke University Press website, and a third set of different results was obtained. It appears that although the corpus remains the same, the tools used to access it must differ. This highlights how imperative it is for forensic linguists to carefully document which search tools have been used as a way to explain discrepancies. When the three words constituting Shuy's set of idiolectal co-selections (*confession, consult, unintentionally*) were entered, as expected, just the two documents originally identified in 2004 as being authored by Shuy were identified.

To demonstrate whether it is possible to identify idiolectal co-selections for other authors, the process for selecting idiolectal co-selections

DOI: 10.1057/9781137413758.0005

was repeated for QD2. However, the feasibility of this approach for QD2 is limited compared to QD1 in that the database used for the targeted search was considerably larger. In fact, the database was so large that all search query results were capped by the database search engine at 200 results. The manifesto was not published in this database, and so, unlike with QD1, it could not be expected to be included in the search results. The range of results returned by the search query therefore was zero at the lowest, and in excess of 200 documents with no specific number given above this total at the highest. For example, *adopt, analogous, compatible,* and *exclude* all occurred in more than 200 documents, whilst words including *exhorts, gratified,* and *predatory* did not occur in any of the documents. Knowing that Kaczynski was the author of QD2, the aim of this exercise was to establish how many lexical items returned other documents authored by Kaczynski.

To this effect, of the 497 lexical items entered separately as search queries, only four produced the desired results – that is, other documents authored by Kaczynski: *contradiction, generated, generates,*[5] and *reversed. Contradiction* returned three separate documents authored by Kaczynski, whilst *generated, generates,* and *reversed* only returned one. This raises two interesting points: firstly, the combination of *contradiction, generated, generates,* and *reversed* did not occur in any single one document, meaning that whilst the words were clearly known to Kaczynski, the exact combination could not be considered to constitute idiolectal co-selections for Kaczynski. Secondly, *contradiction* returned a total of 200+ documents, *generated* returned 200+, *generates* returned 200+, and *reversed* returned 177. It can therefore be concluded that these lexical items are in no way distinctive to this particular author, and furthermore that the identification of co-selections for the author of QD1 appeared to be distinctive only because the targeted searches were carried out on a considerably smaller database. Unlike with QD1, this process was not repeated at a ten-year interval. In 2004, JSTOR searched 15 mathematics journals. In 2014 this number had increased to 259 titles, and whilst the option to select which journals to search specifically, the full range was not available and so a comparable search was not possible.

In light of these results, a more convincing test of authorship will be to determine whether the idiolectal co-selections identified for the author of QD1 can withstand a general web search using commercial search engines. To this end, it is predicted that when searching the web, only

DOI: 10.1057/9781137413758.0005

other documents authored by Shuy should be returned when the search query involves the three lexical items constituting Shuy's set of idiolectal co-selections.

3.3   Web searches using commercial search engines

After all of the lexical items were independently searched in the targeted searches, it was possible to comment on the frequency (and therefore distinctiveness) of each lexical item. For this stage of the analysis, those lexical items which occurred in two or more documents authored by the same author as the QD were considered to be evidence of idiolectal co-selections because occurrence in two or more documents demonstrates that the authors used the combination of those particular lexical items in at least two different documents. The set of idiolectal co-selections for each author was then used as a general web search query and entered into the Google search engine. This search engine was selected because of its size. As discussed in Chapter 2, Section 2.3, Blair, Urland and Ma (2002) advise researchers "to use search engines with large databases … to ensure the greatest representativeness of the frequency estimates" (p. 286), and as Google had one of the largest databases, both in 2004 and in 2014, it was expected that more conclusive evidence would be produced. Search queries were entered using Boolean commands to ensure maximum accuracy, for example, for QD1, the search query was *confession AND consult AND unintentionally* and for QD2, the search query was *contradiction AND generated AND generates AND reversed*. It is hypothesised that if the search query returned only documents by the authors of QD1 and QD2, respectively, then strong evidence of idiolectal co-selections identified using the method outlined in this chapter would hold potential as a marker of authorship.

When the search query for QD1 was entered into the Google UK search engine in 2004, 126 webpages were returned and this included QD1, but unfortunately did not include any other documents authored by Shuy. Knowing already that a set of idiolectal co-selections for Kaczynski was unlikely, the search query for QD2 was also entered into the Google UK search engine. This search returned 5,810 documents, of which only one was identified as being authored by Kaczynski and was in fact a version of QD2.

DOI: 10.1057/9781137413758.0005

The results are disappointing for two reasons. Firstly, the high proportion of returned results means that a process of elimination to identify an author would be unfeasible, that is, a potential 126 – and certainly not 5,810 – authors would be an unacceptable number of candidate authors to present to investigators (e.g. the police, the FBI) for further investigation. Secondly, in both of the examples, only one document was returned by the authors, when it has already been established that Shuy has published at least two documents, and Kacynski has published at least four. Therefore, despite knowing that further documents written by these authors exist on the web, searching the web on this occasion did not guarantee that the documents could be found by the commercial search engines and it is likely that additional documents written by these authors are stored in the hidden web (cf. Chapter 2, Section 2.2) which are beyond the reach of the commercial search engines. These results appear to diminish the power of idiolectal co-selections – certainly based on the method used – because multiple authors may be candidate authors of the QDs.

The Google searches were repeated a decade later. The three idiolectal co-selections identified for Shuy were entered and 8,680,000 results were obtained. However, on closer scrutiny, the search had been widened to include derivatives of these words (as indicated in Chapter 2, Section 2.2), so quotation marks were then used around each individual word to indicate that only these particular words should be matched. This produced 1,530,000 results – a massive increase in comparison to the 126 matches found in 2004. In addition, a caveat appeared with the search results indicating that one result had been removed in response to a complaint received under the US Digital Millennium Copyright Act. Although only a minor point, this serves to highlight how decisions are made about which results to display which go far beyond the searcher's control. Likewise, Kaczynski's set of four idiolectal co-selections were entered to reveal 44,600,000 results, which narrowed to 14,400,000 when the quotation marks were used around individual words. Again, this shows a massive increase compared to 2004 when 5,810 results were obtained. These results are far too high to be useful as evidence of authorship.

The next step is to adopt a different approach to authorship analysis using known writings of candidate authors (suspects) in order to derive a set of idiolectal co-selections. This forms the basis of Chapter 4.

DOI: 10.1057/9781137413758.0005

Notes

1 Whilst numbers were not deemed relevant in this study, other studies may find it useful to take into account the formatting of numbers, such as dates (cf. McMenamin, 2002).

2 Although Carter (1998) does point out that "frequency is no guarantee of coreness" (p. 47).

3 In a pilot version of this work, a British author had been selected to test the methodology. To remove the core vocabulary, a word-frequency list from the British National Corpus (BNC) was used, and the results were disappointing with relatively few words from the BNC list occurring in the text of this author. This raises the question again of representativeness, and how core vocabulary should be determined.

4 Since the searches were repeated in 2014, all four volumes published in 2004 were available for searching unlike in the original searches. All search results were checked and any results for volumes three and four were not included in this analysis to ensure comparability with the original search.

5 Whilst *generated* and *generates* are clearly derivatives of the same lemma, *generate* was not counted as a core word, which explains why these words were not excluded from QD2.

DOI: 10.1057/9781137413758.0005

4

Attributing Documents to Candidate Authors Using Idiolectal Co-selection and the Web

Abstract: *In this chapter, empirical research is described where a Questioned Document is compared to the known writings of three candidate authors, with the aim of establishing whether idiolectal co-selections are a useful marker of authorship and whether the web can be used to generate reliable evidence. Lexical items are identified which are not core words, derivatives of core words or subject-specific words, and which are argued to constitute a set of idiolectal co-selections for each author. Results show that idiolectal co-selections hold some potential as a marker of authorship for prolific authors on the web, but reliability between search engines is low, as is reliability over a period of one week. Attempting to repeat the results after a period of ten years revealed that web searches cannot be repeated exactly, which raises issues for the forensic context.*

Keywords: authorship analysis; idiolectal co-selection; lexis; marker of authorship; reliability of search engines; reliability of web

Larner, Samuel. *Forensic Authorship Analysis and the World Wide Web*. Basingstoke: Palgrave Macmillan, 2014. DOI: 10.1057/9781137413758.0006.

In the previous chapter it was shown that when there are no candidate authors for comparison to a QD, the list of potential authors produced using idiolectal co-selections as a marker of authorship was too high to be useful – 126 for QD1 and 5,810 for QD2. Therefore, in this chapter, a different approach was taken. Often, when forensic linguists are asked to provide evidence for an investigation, a list of candidate authors is provided, along with texts known to have been written by the candidate authors for comparison to the QD (e.g. Eagleson, 1994; Grant, 2010). To replicate this type of situation, in this chapter, one QD is analysed against texts produced by a pool of three candidate authors. As with the previous chapter, the aim of this chapter is to determine whether idiolectal co-selections can be used as a marker of authorship, and whether the web produces reliable evidence.

4.1   Data and method

For this investigation, as with the previous chapter, the Unabomber's terrorist manifesto was used as the QD. In addition, three candidate authors were selected, and for each candidate author, three texts were selected giving a total of nine KDs to compare against the QD. The three candidate authors were Theodore Kaczynski (the Unabomber), Roger Shuy (a professor of linguistics), and Noam Chomsky (also a professor of linguistics). Kaczynski had to be selected as a candidate author since he is the actual author of the QD. Shuy and Chomsky were selected because they were in some respects potentially comparable on sociolinguistic variables (e.g. gender, similar ages, similar education levels). Furthermore, in 2004, Chomsky had published extensively on the visible web, whilst Shuy was largely confined to academic articles in databases (i.e. the hidden web).

The texts were selected by searching online academic databases, specifying each author as the search query. In the JSTOR mathematics database, five documents were identified as authored by Kaczynski; therefore three were selected at random as the known texts (1968a; 1968b; 1969). Only two documents were written by Shuy (2000; 2002), which were downloaded from the online version of the linguistics journal *Journal of American Speech*, and so a third (1996) was selected by extracting the first 1,850 words from one of his books.[1] However, at the time of searching, no articles could be found in academic databases for Chomsky,[2] and so three articles were selected at random from a website (http://zcomm.org/znet/)

DOI: 10.1057/9781137413758.0006

which featured resources for people interested in social change, and which had archived many of his writings (1999; 2001; 2002). All nine KDs were believed to be single authored and not written in collaboration with anyone else, although as published academic journal articles, certainly for Kaczynski and Shuy, there may be textual influence from reviewers, editors, and proof-readers. This is considered further in Chapter 5. All three texts for each candidate author were judged to be in the same genre – that is, Kaczynski's texts were all academic mathematics articles, Shuy's texts were all academic linguistics publications, and Chomsky's texts were all journalistic political writings. The data ranged in terms of length with the QD being the longest document at 34,581 words. The known texts for Kaczynski were approximately[3] 4,300, 1,600, and 1,200; for Shuy, 5,858, 1,170, and 1,850; and for Chomsky, 4,157, 2,402, and 2,600.

The same procedures as described in Chapter 3 were carried out on the nine KDs of the candidate authors; that is, the removal of punctuation, direct quotation, numbers (particularly mathematical formulae in the case of Kaczynski), and citations. Unlike in Chapter 3, derivatives of core words, subject-specific vocabulary, and shared vocabulary between the texts were not removed. In Chapter 3, no candidate authors were available, and so these categories of words were removed as a way to isolate the potentially more distinctive lexis in the texts. The focus in this chapter, however, is on the lexis which appears to be used consistently by an author – something which can be ascertained to some extent because known documents are available. As would be expected, there were many lexical items which occurred not only between the three known writings in each author's sub-corpus, but also across the three sub-corpora, and indeed across all nine KDs. Such words included grammatical words (*the, a, of, on, or,* etc.) and as a consequence, it was necessary to remove the core vocabulary as identified using the 5,000 most frequently occurring words in the Brown Corpus (as outlined in Chapter 3.1) from these documents, on the premise that as they were so common, they were less likely to be distinctive. As in Chapter 3, the focus of interest here is on types and not tokens. Consequently, the sub-corpus for Kaczynski consisted of 963 types; the sub-corpus for Shuy consisted of 2,321 types and the sub-corpus for Chomsky consisted of 2,474 types. An alphabetically sorted word list of the remaining words for each text was then created. The three word lists for each author were compared so that any lexis shared across each group of three known texts for each individual author could be identified. Any such lexical items constituted the lexical co-selections for each

DOI: 10.1057/9781137413758.0006

author. For Kaczynski, 12 lexical items were shared across his three KDs (*assert, boundary, bounded, convergence, deduce, domain, inequality, integer, lemma, real-valued, subset, theorem*), for Shuy, just three (*linguist*, speakers, specialized*), and for Chomsky, a total of five lexical items occurred across all three KDs (*choices, excluded, far, supporters, topic*). As in Chapter 3, if these lexical co-selections can be ascertained to be sufficiently distinctive, this may provide evidence of authorship. The idiolectal co-selections identified for Shuy contain the lemma *linguist** which accounts for the lexical items *linguistic, linguistics,* and *linguist.* It should also be noted that Kaczynski's idiolectal co-selections are heavily dominated by mathematical terminology; Kaczynski's profile is particularly distinctive in this regard compared to the other two authors, which may prove to be problematic. Nonetheless, they will remain in this analysis to demonstrate any potential effect of genre, which is further discussed in Chapter 5.

In order to ascertain the distinctiveness of the lexical co-selections, a series of web searches – both targeted and general – were conducted. The JSTOR mathematics database (1964–9) was used to assess the distinctiveness of the lexis used by Kaczynski, the *Journal of American Speech* was used to assess the distinctiveness of the lexis used by Shuy, whilst for Chomsky, the ZNet archive was used. In each case, these are the sources from where the data were obtained. For the general web searches, the commercial search engines Google and AlltheWeb were used, and the results were repeated in order to test reliability. As in Chapter 3, if the search returned only the source document and preferably other writings by the same author, then strong evidence of the power of idiolectal co-selection may be provided. However, if, as in Chapter 3, a selection of documents are returned which are written by a variety of different authors, then not only will the evidence of idiolectal co-selection be less convincing, but so too will the effectiveness of the web as an authorship analysis tool be called into question.

4.2   Targeted searches

When searching the *American Speech* Journals (2000–4), the set of idiolectal co-selections identified for Shuy returned 15 documents, only two of which were actually authored by Shuy. One explanation for this may be that the words identified as being idiolectally co-selected (*linguist*, speakers, specialized*) are too limited and subject-specific, and so it should come as no surprise when a linguistics journal contains multiple articles with the words *linguistics* and *speakers* in them. The conclusion can be reached that when identifying idiolectal co-selections for an author, subject-specific vocabulary may need to be removed (as in Chapter 3). However, this would have left Shuy with only one lexical item (*specialized*), which would therefore have made it impossible to make conclusions about his authorship. It would also be hard to argue a single lexical item as a co-selection. As with the previous chapter, this process was repeated in 2014 in order to assess the reliability of the results. Searching in this way revealed ten results, a reduction of five compared to 2004, although the two authored by Shuy were still identified.

To further investigate the limitation of idiolectal co-selections based on subject-specific vocabulary, the search query was extended to cover all of the journals held on the academic database, which included journals published in, amongst others, business studies, history, humanities, law, medicine, and social sciences. This wider search query returned 432 documents, of which still only two were written by Shuy. The existence of idiolectal co-selection for this author – based on the data used and the methods outlined in this chapter – is not apparent. It must be borne in mind, however, that Shuy may be a less prolific author on the web. This is discussed further in Chapter 5. Repeating the process in 2014, a total of 10,154 results were identified compared to 432 a decade earlier. This is inevitably due to the increasing size of the database with more and more journals being archived, and of course the fact that an additional ten years of published material was included in the search. The results serve to further dilute the usefulness of something as persuasive as a set of idiolectal co-selections.

The idiolectal co-selections identified for Kaczynski were entered as a search query into the JSTOR academic database, searching all articles published in mathematics journals in the years 1964–9. These 12 idiolectal co-selections produced only three documents, of which two were actually authored by Kaczynski. Encouraged by these results, the search was then extended to include all mathematics articles published in the entire database (dated 1800–2004), and in this instance, only 11 documents were returned, of which the same two by Kaczynski appeared. This result, although not conclusive, is certainly a manageable and encouraging figure for further analysis as a list of 11 candidate authors may be a feasible number to present to the police for further investigation. The search results could not be replicated in 2014 since the JSTOR advanced

DOI: 10.1057/9781137413758.0006

search tool could not accommodate a 12-item query, illustrating again the changing nature of search tools and their lack of longevity.

A promising result was returned for Chomsky, given that his idiolectal co-selections entered as a search query identified 16 documents, of which 14 were separate documents all authored by him. The remaining two were not clearly attributed to any one author, but in either case, did not appear to be attributable to Chomsky. When repeated in 2014, the set of five idiolectal co-selections generated nine results which is a decrease from the 16 identified in 2004. Of the nine results, four were attributed to Chomsky – the three known texts plus an additional new document (Chomsky, 2011). In explaining this discrepancy over the ten-year period, it is possible that ZNet does not keep an updated archive of everything it publishes, and perhaps only keeps documents published between certain dates so that older documents identified in 2004 were not available for searching in 2014.

It should be borne in mind that these search queries were incredibly restricted in scope, and the real test of both idiolectal co-selection as a marker of authorship and the effectiveness of the web as an authorship tool occurs when the idiolectal co-selections are used as search queries in a major commercial search engine, searching many more documents.

4.3   Web searches using commercial search engines

In Chapter 3, the Google search engine was used to perform the web search queries. However, this was not possible for present purposes since, in 2004 when the first stage of analysis was completed, Google limited search queries to only ten words (although in 2014, no such restriction is apparent). This is insufficient since a set of 12 idiolectal co-selections were identified for Kaczynski and so a different search engine had to be selected. The decision was made to use the AltaVista search engine as this allowed for the larger search query. In 2004, AltaVista's database was smaller than Google's, but it was deemed to be acceptable as Fielden and Kuntz (2002) commented that AltaVista "would often get documents the other search engines could not reach" (p. 71) because of the indexing system that it used.

In order to determine the reliability of the AltaVista search engine, and also demonstrate whether the use of different search engines can affect results, the search queries were additionally entered into the AlltheWeb search engine. Furthermore, the search queries for both search engines were replicated seven days later, and ten years later, to begin to demonstrate both short-term and long-term reliability of the web and to establish whether time is a factor which should be considered when using the web as evidence in forensic linguistics. The set of idiolectal co-selections identified for Shuy were entered into the AltaVista search engine, and 9,280 documents were returned from the query, of which none appeared to be authored by Shuy. Replicating the search seven days later, 9,360 documents were returned, an increase of 80 documents, but still no documents authored by Shuy. Kaczynski's set of idiolectal co-selections were entered into the AltaVista search engine, which returned nine documents. Interestingly, seven days later when the search was replicated, still only nine documents were returned, showing that the results were consistent with one another. However, none of the nine documents were authored by Kaczynski. Furthermore, all of these documents were mathematics-based documents, and most certainly, the Unabomber's manifesto was not identified as was predicted. In this way, attributing the QD to its actual author was not possible. The idiolectal co-selections identified for Chomsky also produced disappointing results because 33,700 documents were returned, and although a proportion of these were authored by Chomsky, it was impossible to determine how many documents were actually authored by him due to the high number of results. However, upon inspecting the first 20 documents, 15 were authored by Chomsky, whilst the remaining documents tended not to be. Seven days later, the search was replicated and 34,600 documents were returned (an increase of 900 documents), again with approximately the first 15 documents being authored by Chomsky.

To compare results obtained from different commercial search engines, the searches were replicated using the AlltheWeb search engine, and again one week later. For Shuy, 6,320 documents were returned from the search query in the first instance and 6,410 when the search was replicated one week later showing an increase of 90. None of these documents were authored by Shuy. For Kaczysnki, only two documents were returned, and neither was authored by Kaczynski. One week later, this number rose to seven documents, but again, none were authored by Kaczynski. When Chomsky's set of idiolectal co-selections were entered as a search query, 23,400 documents were returned in the first instance, and one week later, 24,100 documents were returned (an increase of 700 documents), and unfortunately as before, it was impossible to estimate how many of these documents were authored by Chomsky, but

DOI: 10.1057/9781137413758.0006

his presence as an author – and therefore his link with these idiolectal co-selections – was established.

The searches were then repeated in 2014. However, since 2004, AltaVista and AlltheWeb had been acquired by Yahoo!, meaning that the results could not be replicated exactly as they had in 2004. The Yahoo! search engine was used and each author's set of idiolectal co-selections were entered as search queries. A total of 47,300 results were obtained for Shuy, 26,200,000 for Chomsky, and 3,830 for Kaczynski. For each author there has been a dramatic increase in the results obtained, compared to both the AltaVista and the AlltheWeb results carried out a decade earlier. Incidentally, for Chomsky, scrutinising some of the results showed that the search engine had matched *support* instead of *supporters*, and even using quotation marks did not prevent this from happening. For Kaczynski, the first two results were two of the journal articles used as the known documents, although no significance can be attached to this since there is no way to know how these results had been ranked.

In summary, the empirical research carried out in this chapter reveals that whilst some evidence of the power of idiolectal co-selection can be claimed for Chomsky at least, using the web proved to be unreliable. Results varied between search engines and a small amount of variability was observed over a seven day period. More alarmingly, a decade later the results could not be replicated exactly as they had been originally since the search engines had been acquired by another company. This highlights the lack of scrutiny available when using the web to produce evidence since the results from 2004 cannot now be verified. This is potentially concerning from an academic perspective, but even more concerning from a forensic perspective; the inference is that evidence produced at one stage of an investigation or trial may not be available at a later date. This may be particularly salient in the case of appeals where previous evidence is reviewed. In light of these findings, the final chapter attempts to conclude this research by drawing together the main findings and answering the central research question.

Notes

1   It is worth acknowledging that this information relates to the first stage of this research, carried out in 2004. At the time of writing in 2014, 25 sole-authored articles by Shuy were actually available for full-text download.

DOI: 10.1057/9781137413758.0006

2   Although, as with footnote 1, at the time of writing, 82 sole-authored articles were electronically available for Chomsky. Both footnotes 1 and 2 indicate the importance of linguists being aware of the limitations of their resources. The discrepancy between 2004 and 2014 totals is likely due to the fact that academic databases have increased the number of archived, full-text material they store, and potentially the fact that the research has been carried out using resources available at two different universities.

3   The total words in each document for Kaczynski only were estimated. The documents were so old that the downloadable .pdf files were images of the original document, rather than files which could be copied into a word document and which contained a good many statistical equations and formulae, so an accurate word count was difficult to establish.

DOI: 10.1057/9781137413758.0006

5
The Suitability of the Web for Producing Forensic Evidence

Abstract: *In an attempt to assess whether idiolectal co-selection can be used as a marker of authorship, and whether the web can reliably be used as forensic evidence, this chapter summarises findings from empirical research. The UNABOM investigation is discussed and analysis carried out which reveals that whilst at the time idiolectal co-selection was argued to be a powerful marker of authorship, the present research suggests otherwise. Due to the unreliable nature of search engines, the range of search optimisation techniques that are applied to search results, and the commercial nature of search engines, this research concludes by cautioning forensic linguists over the use of the web in forensic investigations and calls for further research and debate in this area.*

Keywords: authorship analysis; forensic linguistics; idiolect; idiolectal co-selection; Unabomber; web as corpus

Larner, Samuel. *Forensic Authorship Analysis and the World Wide Web.* Basingstoke: Palgrave Macmillan, 2014. DOI: 10.1057/9781137413758.0007.

DOI: 10.1057/9781137413758.0007

This is only a small-scale study which is limited in scope. It does not, for instance, reflect the myriad ways in which the web can be used in forensic linguistics, or even forensic authorship attribution. Therefore, caution must be exercised in considering the results. This study does, nonetheless, serve to highlight some of the issues inherent in using the web to produce evidence in a forensic context and in this chapter, such issues will be discussed. Before doing so, it may be useful to recap the main findings from the empirical work described in Chapters 3 and 4 which attempted to better understand whether (a) idiolectal co-selection is useful as a marker of authorship, and (b) whether the web is reliable enough to produce evidence of idiolectal co-selection in a forensic context.

In Chapter 3, two QDs were under investigation when no KDs written by candidate authors were available for comparison. Using a method specifically developed for this research, a small set of words was identified for each document which were argued to be idiolectal co-selections for each QD's author. The following results were obtained:

▶ It was possible to determine a set of words which were idiolectal to the author of each QD. For QD1 (Shuy), these were *confession, consult,* and *construe,* whilst for QD2 (Kaczynski), they were *contradiction, generated, generates,* and *reversed*;

▶ When the idiolectal co-selections were used as search queries in targeted searches, the results were promising, and seemed to provide some – albeit limited – evidence of authorship for the author of QD1;

▶ However, when these sets of idiolectal co-selections were used as search queries on the web, too many results were returned, making it impossible to determine only one possible author of the questioned documents; and

▶ When the analysis was repeated a decade later, far too many results were generated by the search engines to be able to say anything meaningful about the authorship of either QD.

Chapter 4 outlined an alternative approach in which a QD was analysed with a group of three candidate authors. The web was used to assess the distinctiveness of the idiolectal co-selections with the following results:

▶ Targeted searches appeared to provide stronger evidence of authorship than web searches using commercial search engines,

DOI: 10.1057/9781137413758.0007

particularly for Chomsky whose writings – both KDs and an additional document – were identified using his set of idiolectal co-selections;

▸ However, it was not possible to determine the author of the QD using idiolectal co-selections as identified through the method outlined, and the web;

▸ The results returned by the search engines varied between themselves;

▸ The results returned by the search engines varied when conducted seven days later; and

▸ The results returned by the search engines showed further substantial variation when conducted ten years later.

The empirical research carried out reveals a great deal about idiolectal co-selection as a marker of authorship, and the extent to which the web can be used as an evidential tool. In Chapter 3, it was shown that no other documents, other than the QDs for the authors of QD1 and QD2, were identified by the search queries and this highlights the problem of the hidden web, and linked to this, is the problem that the authors may not have actually published to any great extent on the web. Additionally, Chapter 4 revealed that the large number of documents returned by the search queries for one of the candidate authors – Chomsky – highlights the problem of using such a large database (in this case, the web), and, as was also shown in Chapter 4, the very specific genre of the documents used in the Kaczynski sub-corpus seems to have had implications for the search results in that topic-related matches were predominant in the search results. Furthermore, both empirical chapters demonstrated that as time progresses, search engines produce ever-changing results. Based on the findings derived from the empirical research, it is now possible to investigate the evidence of idiolectal co-selection as it was outlined in Chapter 1 – that is, that idiolectal co-selections were distinctive to the Unabomber when searching the web.

5.1   UNABOM revisited

To recap from Chapter 1, the 12 words and phrases highlighted in the UNABOM trial were *at any rate, clearly, in practice, gotten, more or less, moreover, on the other hand, presumably, propaganda, thereabouts,* and

DOI: 10.1057/9781137413758.0007

lexemes derived from the lemmas *argu* and *propos*. It was claimed that 69 documents were found on the web which contained all 12 words and phrases. In order to assess whether, as in the original trial, 69 documents – all versions of the manifesto – were still identified by a search engine, these 12 words and phrases were entered into the Google search engine in 2014, and a total of 184,000 matches were identified. Google automatically filtered this search to only show 17 results since the majority were duplicates, a clear example of search optimisation. Inspecting these 17 results revealed that several matches were in fact other academic texts describing the UNABOM evidence, and so the 12 words and phrases were being used in exactly the same way as in this publication. The remaining matches included a transport bill, a Wikipedia entry on creationism, an electronic version of an edited collection on the topic of modern literature, an electronic version of an edited collection of essays related to national security and defence, and an e-book aimed at reporters and journalists outlining how to write feature articles. Only one match was a copy of the Unabomber's terrorist manifesto. In this context, the argument that something as powerful as idiolectal co-selection appears to be weakened, and Lakoff's position that any text which argues a position could be expected to include such words and phrases appears to be strengthened. Both Woolls and Coulthard (1998) and Johnson (1997) argue that plagiarism can be detected by identifying lexical overlap, and in this respect, searching the web for 12 words and phrases and finding exactly the same document and no others may in fact have been akin to the methods used for identifying plagiarism, which, due to the limited nature of the web at the time, looked more persuasive than it actually was.

5.2   Idiolectal co-selection as a marker of authorship

Previous research into authorship attribution has often used documents (both QDs and KDs) which are written in the same genre. For example, Johnson (1997) used student essays written on the same topic, whilst Hänlein (1999) used essays from *Time Magazine*. The process for identifying a set of idiolectal co-selections for each author should, to some extent at least, have meant that the set of idiolectal co-selections was less related to topic and more likely to occur in any text written by that particular author. However, based on the results returned by the search engines, what actually happened was that the idiolectal co-selections for each

DOI: 10.1057/9781137413758.0007

author attracted documents authored both by the particular author, along with documents written by other authors but *on a similar topic*. For example, even though Kaczynski is known to be the author of the Unabomber's terrorist manifesto, when the set of idiolectal co-selections identified for him was used in search queries, only mathematics documents published by other authors were returned (as shown in Chapter 4). This suggests that the set of idiolectal co-selections identified for Kaczynski was too deterministic in that it attracted a certain genre, rather than characterising his idiolect.

This problem with the method is further illustrated with the set of idiolectal co-selections identified for Chomsky in Chapter 4. Even though the set of idiolectal co-selections identified for him returned the most interesting and promising results, it should be noted that only his political writings were recognised by the search query, and none of his other writings were found (e.g. his work in the field of linguistics). This may be for two reasons: firstly, it is possible that only his political works are in the public domain, whilst his academic writings are published in the hidden areas of the web which general search engines could not find. Secondly, it is possible that, like Kaczynski, his set of idiolectal co-selections was too deterministic and that the idiolectal co-selections were indicative of his political writing style, which perhaps differs from the idiolectal co-selections he may use when writing on different topics or in a different genre. This then leads to the question of whether authorial style is constant across genres – a question which warrants considerably more research and cannot be answered within the confines of the current research.

In Chapter 2, Section 1.2, it was argued that lexis is an appropriate and accepted marker of authorship. In the context of the present research, it should be remembered that a small selection of lexical items were shared between documents authored by the same person (those identified as idiolectal co-selections, in fact) which therefore demonstrates consistent authorial choices or habits. As such, this does seem to support the evidence of lexis being an appropriate marker of authorship. The question of how stable lexis is as a marker of authorship though remains to be answered. This is not least because of the problem stated by Hoover (2003), that "authors normally learn new words. Authors also forget words, or stop using them" (p. 157) and also by Love (2002) who comments that "[f]avorite words are not always permanent even in the work of a particular author" (p. 108).

DOI: 10.1057/9781137413758.0007

In considering this issue, it is important to recognise that all of the texts used for analysis in Chapter 4 were from similar periods of time. For Kaczynski, his KDs were published in 1968 and 1969, Chomsky's KDs were published in 1999, 2001, and 2002, and Shuy's KDs represented the biggest span of six years, being published in 1996, 2000, and 2002. Despite being the longest span, some positive results were obtained for Shuy's set of idiolectal co-selection in the targeted searches carried out in Chapter 3. Likewise, the analysis conducted on Chomsky's KDs in Chapter 4 showed a high degree of consistency between the lexis of all three texts in the Chomsky sub-corpus, and then with the wider range of documents produced by Chomsky when his set of idiolectal co-selections was used in a general web search query. It should be borne in mind, however, that dates cited refer to publication dates and are not necessarily the dates when the texts were authored and so this study cannot make strong claims about the stability of lexis over time.

Some consideration must also be paid to the actual method used for attributing documents to their authors. A valid criticism of this work is that it is very restricted in scope. It has not, for instance, considered other lexical markers of authorship including an analysis of standard and non-standard spellings, frequency of function words, average word lengths, and so on. Nor does this research explore authorial patterns in the use of phrases. Kjellmer (1991) argues that there is a tendency "for speakers of a language to arrange words in groups and to use the same arrangement whenever the need arises rather than to rearrange the words or to choose alternative ways of expression" (p. 114). In essence, whilst Kjellmer does not explicitly state it, if authors routinely relied on particular phrases, these could be indicative of authorship, and future studies may wish to adopt this approach, although a preliminary investigation into the use of fixed phrases as a marker of authorship suggests this may not be an entirely fruitful marker of authorship (cf. Larner, 2014).

Love (2002) explicates the notion of collaborative authorship as different to single authorship. Single authorship for Love is "creating a text in solitariness" (p. 33). Love explains that this is because single authorship:

> [O]mits ... all that precedes the act of writing (language acquisition, education, experiences, conversation, reading of other authors); likewise everything that follows the phase of initial inscription while the work is vetted by friends and advisers, receives second thought and improvements, is edited for the press, if that is its destination, and given the material form in which it will encounter its readers. (p. 33)

DOI: 10.1057/9781137413758.0007

The documents used as KDs in Chapter 4 were mainly those of collaborative authorship (by Love's definition) in that they were almost certainly proof-read, subjected to peer-review, and edited. Quite what the effect of an editor or proof-reader has on an individual author's idiolectal choices and habits remains to be determined. Indeed, the notion of authorship on the web itself deserves further attention. Lanier (2010, cited in Naughton, 2012) explains that Google's aim to digitise every book ever published – known as the Google Books project – creates a blurring at the boundaries of authorship:

> If the books in the cloud are accessed via user interfaces that encourage mashups of fragments that obscure the context and authorship of each fragment, there will be only one book. This is what happens today with a lot of content; often you don't know where a quoted fragment from a news story comes from, who wrote a comment, or who shot a video. (pp. 154–5)

Indeed, Foster (2001) makes the same point:

> In our age of electronic communication and no-holds-barred publication on the Internet … we seem to be constructing a postmodern culture from which the "major author" has evaporated, leaving only text, and more text, billions of words, millions of authors, no matter who's speaking and almost no way of finding out who is. (p. 301)

From this point of view then, it becomes necessary to question whether the notion of idiolect can actually exist on the web or whether such a notion becomes redundant in a sphere where multi-authored documents become more prevalent than traditional single-authored documents. In Chapter 2, Section 2.1, the transition from Web 1.0 to Web 2.0 was described, with the former being a read-only medium, and the latter relying on web users to create and edit content. In light of Lanier (2010) and Foster's (2001) claims, it is conceivable that as web interaction further increases, the notion of a single author may become further distilled in future iterations of the web.

5.3   Using the web as a corpus for producing forensic evidence

When considering the use of the web for generating forensic linguistics evidence, the first issue to consider is the fact that some authors, who are known to have published on the web, are seemingly hidden from the

DOI: 10.1057/9781137413758.0007

commercial search engines – in other words, the places where they have published can be classed as the hidden web. Chapter 3 clearly demonstrates this phenomenon when the known writings of Kaczynski (from a mathematics database) and the known writings of Shuy (from a linguistics database) were not identified in the general web search queries. Therefore, if a forensic linguist is using the web to find an author, they have no guarantee that a general search engine will necessarily identify all of the relevant documents. Publishing on the web, therefore, is not the same as publishing in areas of the hidden web, and any analysis carried out using the web as a tool needs to acknowledge this limitation. If it is not possible to ascertain where an author has actually published, the analysis is subject to chance and this is in no way satisfactory in the forensic linguistics arena. This finding is in line with Lindquist and Levin (2000) who argue that restrictions imposed on corpora mean that research can be conducted with insufficient and unrepresentative material, which raises the question again of just how representative the web is, and what exactly it represents, as discussed in Chapter 2, Section 2.4. Whilst issues in the use of corpora, particularly of availability and cost, may be eradicated by using the web, the researcher is still limited by the abilities of the search engines used – after all, they do not cover the whole web. Some authors may be prolific writers in some areas of the web but unless those areas are publicly accessible, commercial search engines will not be able to locate them.

The problem with authors publishing only in the hidden areas of the web is further exacerbated by non-existent authors; that is, authors who have not published on the web at all. Whilst there are undoubtedly innumerable authors who do publish on the web (both in the hidden and general areas), there is still a large group of people who have published nothing. The discussion in Chapter 2, Section 2.4 highlighted that if the web is to be viewed as a corpus, it cannot be representative of literally "everyone's language" (Blair, Urland & Ma, 2002: 287) because of the fact that not everybody has published something on the web, and of those that have, there is no guarantee that commercial search engines will be able to locate such documents. The conclusion can therefore be reached that the web can never be conclusive in analyses of authorship until every author in the world has published several documents to the web and until the search engines have the capacity to search all of those documents, which seems like an unlikely target for the near future at least.

In Chapter 2, Section 2.3, the research carried out by Blair, Urland and Ma (2002), who conducted research to examine word frequency results from search engines, was described. They found that the results from the search engines demonstrated consistency with one another and furthermore, that when they replicated their results six months later, the results were also consistent, yet this seems to conflict directly with the results presented throughout this research. The comparisons of word search frequencies varied (often hugely) not only between different search engines, but also between the seven-day and ten-year periods over which the searches were conducted. A difference between the present research and that of Blair, Urland and Ma is that they were looking at the frequencies of individual words, whilst the present research was in some instances working with combinations of words. A reason why this should make a difference is, regrettably, not forthcoming. A possible explanation may be that Blair, Urland and Ma conducted their research in 2002, and it is possible that in the two years between their research and the start of the empirical work carried out in this project, and certainly in the intervening decade, the web growth has accelerated to the extent that perhaps in 2002 the web was in less flux over a six-month period than it was after that period. Certainly, more research in this area is warranted. For present purposes, when using the web for authorship attribution purposes, there needs to be some level of agreement regarding how valid and reliable the results are (particularly if the evidence is to be used in court). A conclusive opinion in this regard is not possible based on the small-scale study presented here but it is certainly hoped that some areas of concern have been raised.

A further issue related to reliability which arises from this research, relates to the availability of tools at a later date. In Chapter 2, Section 2.3, the point was made that Rayson, Charles and Auty (2012) were unable to repeat some of their analyses at a later date because the commercial search engine they used started to charge money for what had previously been a free service. Likewise, in Chapter 4, a similar point was made that the analyses could not be repeated in 2014 in exactly the same way as in 2004 because the search engines originally used had been acquired by another company. It was also explained in Chapter 2, Section 2.2 that how search engines operate is constantly being updated and search queries are constantly optimised to give the user the best possible web searching experience. Coupled with this is the fact that a great deal of what search engines actually do is kept secret in order to protect the commercial interests of the search engine companies. This all points to the fact that web search queries are not replicable under exactly the same

DOI: 10.1057/9781137413758.0007

conditions. Producing forensic evidence under these conditions should perhaps be viewed with scepticism.

Whilst this research set out to explore whether the web can be used as a large corpus for authorship purposes, what has become apparent from the analysis is that it is not a single large corpus; rather it is a culmination of many different, smaller corpora (such as newsgroups, academic texts, and commercial sites) many of which have restricted access, making it impossible to search the whole of the web with one search engine. Viewing the web as a series of smaller, specialised corpora may be more beneficial than assuming that the web is one huge, general corpus, especially since the results presented in Chapters 3 and 4 demonstrate more positive results when smaller, more targeted (and perhaps representative) sections of the web are used. Quite promising results were returned when searches were conducted in the academic journals, whereas when those same searches were conducted with the general commercial search engines, the results were of little practical use because the number of web pages identified as meeting the search criteria was often so huge. So much so, that it could not even be ascertained how much any one author had actually published on the web. This contradicts the argument presented in Chapter 2, Section 1.3 that the larger a database is, the easier it should be to identify an author (Foster, 2001) and seems to support Hoover's (2003) position that accuracy in identifying an author is reduced when vocabulary is used as a marker of authorship with larger databases.

5.4   Conclusion

This research has demonstrated some of the limitations of using the web in cases of authorship attribution and has aimed to demonstrate the practicality of doing so. The outcome of the research was that for small, targeted searches, some promising results could be ascertained, but candidate authors were required. When the searches were conducted on a larger scale (i.e. as much of the web as the commercial search engines had indexed), the results were less promising. In assessing the effectiveness of the web as an evidential tool in cases of authorship attribution, the lack of reliability of search engine results combined with the fact that the linguist cannot be sure of what has actually been searched raises serious questions about the extent to which the web should be used in

DOI: 10.1057/9781137413758.0007

producing forensic evidence. This study also highlights the problem of using a corpus that is too big, with the resulting searches from commercial search engines being too big to be manageable – a situation which worsened when the searches were repeated a decade later.

By returning to Coulthard (1994), it becomes evident how important it is to have reference corpora by which to make generalisations about idiosyncrasies and distinctiveness, and the web, whilst appearing to be a suitable reference corpus, lacks the stability and rigour of other carefully constructed corpora. It is therefore questionable whether the web should be regarded an invaluable tool in the forensic context. The implications of this research suggest that the web is not an effective tool in forensic authorship attribution, because the results need to be replicable. By the time a case reaches court, the analysis carried out using the web is likely to be outdated and inaccurate. Perhaps the most important message then is made by Leech (2007) who cautions that "while the internet is an added resource of immense potential, it does not remove the need to improve and update other textual resources, and does not render obsolete the corpus compiled according to design and systematic sampling" (p. 145).

Fletcher (2007) argues that as "practices evolve to ensure the integrity of web data" using the web "will become fully accepted as a legitimate source for linguistic research" (p. 38). This invites reflection on whether linguistic research carried out using the web is legitimate for producing forensic evidence. The following quotation from Hundt, Nesslehauf and Biewer (2007) neatly summarises the issue:

> [W]e still know very little about the size of this [web] "corpus", the text types it contains, the quality of the material included or the amount of repetitive "junk" that it "samples". Furthermore, due to the ephemeral nature of the web, replicability of the results is impossible. Other problems have to do with the way that the commercial crawlers work: they cannot access all web pages because some pages are "invisible", and – more worrying still – the commercial crawlers have an inbuilt local bias. This poses a real problem if you want to do a manual post-editing of the first several hundred hits of a search, for instance. Commercial crawlers apparently prioritize hits that are closer to the "home" of the individual user, which may lead to different results depending on whether the web is accessed from Britain, the US or Australia ... Crawlers also build up a profile of the user and since we rarely use crawlers for linguistic searches only, this may produce an additional skewing effect. All this adds up to the rather uncomfortable impression that in the web-as-corpus-approach, *the machine is determining the results in a most "unlinguistic" fashion over which we have little or no control.* (pp. 2–3, *my emphasis*)

DOI: 10.1057/9781137413758.0007

Is it acceptable to produce any evidence – let alone evidence used as part of a forensic investigation – in which a computer has determined the results in such an unprincipled, unexplainable, unaccountable, and unrepeatable way? Clearly far more research is required. But hopefully the debate about whether the web should be used as a corpus in forensic investigations can begin.

DOI: 10.1057/9781137413758.0007

Bibliography

Bagavandas, M., & Manimannon, G. (2008) Style Consistency and Authorship Attribution: A Statistical Investigation. *Journal of Quantitative Linguistics*, 15(1), 100–10.

Baker, J. (1988) Pace: A Test of Authorship Based on the Rate at Which New Words Enter an Author's Text. *Literary and Linguistic Computing*, 3(1), 36–9.

Barlow, M. (2010) Individual Usage: A Corpus-Based Study of Idiolects. Paper Presented at LAUD *Conference*, Landau. [WWW] http://michaelbarlow.com/barlowLAUD/pdf [Accessed: August, 2012].

Bel, N., Queralt Estevez, S., Spassova, M. S., & Turell, M. T. (2012) The Use of Sequences of Linguistic Categories in Forensic Written Text Comparison Revisited. In S. Tomblin, N. MacLeod, R. Sousa-Silva, & M. Coulthard (eds), *Proceedings of the International Association of Forensic Linguists' Tenth Biennial Conference*. Aston University, Birmingham, UK: The Centre for Forensic Linguistics, 192–209.

Blair, I., Urland, G., & Ma, J. (2002) Using Internet Search Engines to Estimate Word Frequency. *Behaviour Research Methods, Instruments & Computers*, 34(2), 286–90.

Bloch, B. (1948) A Set of Postulates for Phonemic Analysis. *Language*, 24, 3–46.

Blum, A. (2012) *Tubes: Behind the Scenes at the Internet*. London: Penguin Books Ltd.

Carter, R. (1998) *Vocabulary: Applied Linguistic Perspectives* (2nd Edition). London: Routledge.

DOI: 10.1057/9781137413758.0008

Čermák, F. (2002) Today's Corpus Linguistics: Some Open Questions. *International Journal of Corpus Linguistics*, 7(2), 265–82.

Chaski, C. (2001) Empirical Evaluations of Language-Based Author Identification. *Forensic Linguistics: The International Journal of Speech, Language and the Law*, 8(1), 1–65.

Chomsky, N. (1999) *World Order and Its Rules: U.S. Contempt for the Framework of World Order Is so Extreme There Is Little Left to Discuss.* [WWW] http://zcomm.org/zmagazine/world-order-and-its-rules-by-noam-chomsky/ [Accessed: August, 2014].

Chomsky, N. (2001) *Elections 2000.* [WWW] http://zcomm.org/zmagazine/elections-2000-by-noam-chomsky/ [Accessed: August, 2014].

Chomsky, N. (2002) *The War in Afghanistan.* [WWW] http://zcomm.org/zmagazine/the-war-in-afghanistan-by-noam-chomsky/ [Accessed: August, 2014].

Chomsky, N. (2011) *On Libya and the Unfolding Crises.* [WWW] http://zcomm.org/znetarticle/noam-chomsky-on-libya-and-the-unfolding-crises-by-noam-chomsky/ [Accessed: August, 2014].

Coulthard, M. (1994) On the Use of Corpora in the Analysis of Forensic Texts. *Forensic Linguistics*, 1(1), 27–44.

Coulthard, M. (2000) Whose Text Is It? on the Linguistic Investigation of Authorship. In S. Sarangi, & M. Coulthard (eds), *Discourse and Social Life*. Essex: Pearson Education Limited, 270–87.

Coulthard, M. (2004) Author Identification, Idiolect and Linguistic Uniqueness. *Applied Linguistics*, 25(4), 431–47.

Eagleson, R. (1994) Forensic Analysis of Personal Written Texts: A Case Study. In J. Gibbons (ed.), *Language and the Law*. London: Longman, 362–73.

Eder, M. (2013) Mind Your Corpus: Systematic Errors in Authorship Attribution. *Literary and Linguistic Computing*, 28(4), 603–14.

Fielden, N., & Kuntz, L. (2002) *Search Engines Handbook*. London: McFarland & Company, Inc. Publishers.

Fitzgerald, J. R. (2004) Using a Forensic Linguistic Approach to Track the Unabomber. In J. H. Campbell, & D. Denivi (eds), *Profilers*. New York. Prometheus Books, 193–221.

Fletcher, W. (2007) Concordancing the Web: Promise and Problems, Tools and Techniques. In M. Hundt, N. Nesselhauf, & C. Biewer (eds), *Corpus Linguistics and the Web*. Amsterdam: Rodopi, 25–45.

Foster, D. (2001) *Author Unknown: On the Trail of Anonymous*. London: Macmillan Publishers Ltd.

DOI: 10.1057/9781137413758.0008

Francis, W. N., & Kučera, H. (1979) *Brown Corpus Manual: Manual of Information to Accompany a Standard Corpus of Present-Day Edited American English, for Use with Digital Computers*. [WWW] http:// helmer.aksis.uib.no/icame/brown/bcm.html [Accessed: August, 2004].

Gibbons, J. (2003) *Forensic Linguistics: An Introduction to Language in the Justice System*. Oxford: Blackwell.

Grant, T. (2010) Text Messaging Forensics: Txt 4n6: Idiolect Free Authorship Analysis? In M. Coulthard, & A. Johnson (eds), *The Routledge Handbook of Forensic Linguistics*. Abingdon, Oxford: Routledge, 508–22.

Grieve, J. (2007) Quantitative Authorship Attribution: An Evaluation of Techniques. *Literary and Linguistic Computing*, 22(3), 251–70.

Hänlein, H. (1999) *Studies in Authorship Recognition – A Corpus-Based Approach*. Frankfurt: Peter Lang.

Hockett, C. (1958) *A Course in Modern Linguistics*. New York: The Macmillan Company.

Holmes, D., & Forsyth, R. (1995) The *Federalist* Revisited: New Directions in Authorship Attribution. *Literary and Linguistic Computing*, 10(2), 111–27.

Hoover, D. (2003) Another Perspective on Vocabulary Richness. *Computers and the Humanities*, 37(2), 151–78.

Hundt, M., Nesslehauf, N., & Biewer, C. (2007) Corpus Linguistics and the Web. In M. Hundt, N. Nesselhauf, & C. Biewer (eds), *Corpus Linguistics and the Web*. Amsterdam: Rodopi, 1–5.

Hunston, S. (2002) *Corpora in Applied Linguistics*. Cambridge: Cambridge University Press.

Johnson, A. (1997) Textual Kidnapping – a Case of Plagiarism Among Three Student Texts? *Forensic Linguistics*, 4(2), 210–23.

Kaczynski, T. J. (1968a) Boundary Functions and Sets of Curvilinear Convergence for Continuous Functions. *Transactions of the American Mathematical Society*, 141, 107–25.

Kaczynski, T. J. (1968b) Boundary Functions for Bounded Harmonic Functions. *Transactions of the American Mathematical Society*, 137, 203–9.

Kaczynski, T. J. (1969) The Set of Curvilinear Convergence of a Continuous Function Defined in the Interior of a Cube. *Proceedings of the American Mathematical Society*, 23(2), 323–7.

Kilgarriff, A., & Grefenstette, G. (2003) Introduction to the Special Issue on the Web as Corpus. *Computational Linguistics*, 29(3), 333–47.

DOI: 10.1057/9781137413758.0008

Kjellmer, G. (1991) A Mint of Phrases. In K. Aijmer, & B. Altenberg (eds), *English Corpus Linguistics: Studies in Honour of Jan Svartvik*. London: Longman, 111–27.

Kniffka, H. (2007) *Working in Language and Law: A German Perspective*. Basingstoke: Palgrave Macmillan.

Koetsier, J. (2013) *How Google Searches 30 Trillion Web Pages 100 Billion Times a Month*. [WWW] http://venturebeat.com/2013/03/01/how-google-searches-30-trillion-web-pages-100-billion-times-a-month/ [Accessed: July, 2014].

Kredens, K. (2001) Towards a Corpus-Based Methodology of Forensic Authorship Attribution: A Comparative Study of Two Idiolects. In B. Lewandowska-Tomaszxzyk (ed.), *PALC 2001: Practical Applications in Language Corpora*. Frankfurt: Peter Lang, 405–46.

Kredens, K. (2002) Idiolect in Forensic Authorship Attribution. In P. Stalmaszczyk (ed.), *Folia Linguistica Anglica*, Vol. 4. Lodz: Lodz University Press, 191–212.

Labov, W. (1972) *Sociolinguistic Patterns*. Oxford: Basil Blackwell.

Lanier, J. (2010) *Web 2.0 is Utterly Pathetic* [WWW] http://www.independent.co.uk/life-style/gadgets-and-tech/features/jaron-lanier-web-20-is-utterly-pathetic-1894257.html/ [Accessed: August, 2014].

Larner, S. (2014) A Preliminary Investigation into the Use of Fixed Formulaic Sequences as a Marker of Authorship. *The International Journal of Speech, Language and the Law*, 21(1), 1–22.

Leech, G. (1991) The State of the Art in Corpus Linguists. In K. Aijmer, & B. Altenberg (eds), *English Corpus Linguistics: Studies in Honour of Jan Svartvik*. London: Longman, 8–29.

Leech, G. (2007) New Resources, or Just Better Old Ones? the Holy Grail of Representativeness. In M. Hundt, N. Nesselhauf, & C. Biewer (eds), *Corpus Linguistics and the Web*. Amsterdam: Rodopi, 133–49.

Levene, M. (2010) *Introduction to Search Engines and Web Navigation* (2nd Edition). London: Wiley.

Lindquist, H., & Levin, M. (2000) Apples and Oranges: On Comparing Data from Different Corpora. In C. Mair, & M. Hundt (eds), *Corpus Linguistics and Linguistic Theory: Papers from the Twentieth Conference on English Language Research on Computerized Corpora (ICAME 20) Freiburg im Breisgau 1999*. Amsterdam: Rodopi B.V., 201–14.

Loakes, D. (2006) A Forensic Phonetic Investigation into the Speech Patterns of Identical and Non-Identical Twins. *The International Journal of Speech, Language and the Law*, 15(1), 97–100.

DOI: 10.1057/9781137413758.0008

Louwerse, M. (2004) Semantic Variation in Idiolect and Sociolect: Corpus Linguistic Evidence from Literary Texts. *Computers and the Humanities*, 38, 207–21.

Love, H. (2002) *Attributing Authorship: An Introduction.* Cambridge: Cambridge University Press.

Lüdeling, A., Evert, S., & Baroni, M. (2007) Using Web Data for Linguistics Purposes. In M. Hundt, N. Nesselhauf, & C. Biewer (eds), *Corpus Linguistics and the Web.* Amsterdam: Rodopi, 7–24.

McEnery, T., & Wilson, A. (1996) *Corpus Linguistics.* Edinburgh: Edinburgh University Press.

McMenamin, G. (2002) *Forensic Linguistics: Advances in Forensic Stylistics.* London: CRC Press.

Mello, M. (1999) *The United States of America Versus Theordore John Kaczynski: Ethics, Power and the Invention of the Unabomber.* New York: Context Books.

Miniwatts Marketing Group (2014) *Internet World Stats: Usage and Population Statistics.* [WWW] http://www.internetworldstats.com/stats.htm [Accessed: August, 2014].

Mosteller, F., & Wallace, D. (1963) Inference in an Authorship Problem: A Comparative Study of Discrimination Methods Applied to the Authorship of the Disputed *Federalist* papers. *Journal of the American Statistical Association*, 302(58), 275–309.

Naughton, J. (2012) *What You Really Need to Know About the Internet: From Gutenberg to Zuckerberg.* London: Quercus.

Ntoulas, A., Cho, J., & Olston, C. (2004) What's New on the Web? the Evolution of the Web from a Search Engine Perspective. *WWW2004: The Thirteenth International World Wide Web Conference.* [WWW] http://www2004.wwwconference.org/docs/1p1.pdf [Accessed: August, 2014], 1–12.

Rayson, P., Charles, O., & Auty, I. (2012) Can Google Count? Estimating Search Engine Result Consistency. In A. Kilgarriff, & S. Sharoff (eds), *Proceedings of the Seventh Web as Corpus Workshop (WAC7).* [WWW] *https://sigwac.org.uk/raw-attachment/wiki/WAC7/wac7-proc.pdf [Accessed: August, 2014],* 23–30.

Rosenbach, A. (2007) Exploring Constructions on the Web: A Case Study. In M. Hundt, N. Nesselhauf, & C. Biewer (eds), *Corpus Linguistics and the Web.* Amsterdam: Rodopi, 167–90.

Sapir, E. (1927) Speech as a Personality Trait. *American Journal of Sociology*, 32(6), 892–905.

DOI: 10.1057/9781137413758.0008

Schäfer, R., & Bildhauer, F. (2013) *Web Corpus Construction*. San Francisco: Morgan & Claypool Publishers.

Shuy, R. (1996) *Language Crimes: Use and Abuse of Language Evidence in the Court Room*. Oxford: Blackwell.

Shuy, R. (2000) Keeping Our Tools Sharp and Knowing Where to Use Them. *American Speech*, 75(3), 241–4.

Shuy, R. (2002) A Lexicography Legacy of Fred Cassidy: Forensic Linguistics. *American Speech*, 77(4), 344–57.

Sinclair, J. (1991) *Corpus, Concordance, Collocation*. Oxford: Oxford University Press.

Solan, L., & Tiersma, P. (2004) Author Identification in American Courts. *Applied Linguistics*, 25(4), 448–65.

Stubbs, M. (1986) *Educational Linguistics*. Oxford: Basil Blackwell.

Stubbs, M. (2002) Two Quantitative Methods of Studying Phraseology in English. *International Journal of Corpus Linguistics*, 7(2), 215–44.

Tomblin, S. (2013) 'To Cut a Long Story Short': An Analysis of Formulaic Sequences in Short Written Narratives and Their Potential as Markers of Authorship, Unpublished PhD, Birmingham: Aston University.

Trudgill, P. (1974) *Sociolinguistics: An Introduction to Language and Society*. London: Penguin Books Ltd.

Trudgill, P. (2003) *A Glossary of Sociolinguistics*. Edinburgh: Edinburgh University Press.

Volk, M. (2002) *Using the Web as Corpus for Linguistic Research*. [WWW] http://www.halskov.net/files/Volk_Web_as_Corpus.pdf [Accessed: August, 2014].

Wardhaugh, R. (2006) *An Introduction to Sociolinguistics* (5th Edition). Oxford: Blackwell Publishing.

Winter, E. (1996) The Statistics of Analysing Very Short Texts in a Criminal Context. In H. Kniffka (ed.), *Recent Developments in Forensic Linguistics*. Frankfurt: Peter Lang, 141–79.

Woolls, D., & Coulthard, M. (1998) Tools for the Trade. *Forensic Linguistics*, 5(1), 33–57.

DOI: 10.1057/9781137413758.0008

Index

DOI: 10.1057/9781137413758.0009

GPSR Compliance
The European Union's (EU) General Product Safety Regulation (GPSR) is a set
of rules that requires consumer products to be safe and our obligations to
ensure this.

If you have any concerns about our products, you can contact us on

ProductSafety@springernature.com

In case Publisher is established outside the EU, the EU authorized
representative is:

Springer Nature Customer Service Center GmbH
Europaplatz 3
69115 Heidelberg, Germany